QUIET TIMES WITH GOD

Devotions by
William A. Lauterbach

NORTHWESTERN PUBLISHING HOUSE
Milwaukee, Wisconsin

Second printing, 2018

Cover Photo: Unsplash
Art Director: Karen Knutson
Design Team: Diane Cook and Pam Dunn

All Scripture quotations, unless otherwise indicated, are taken from the HOLY BIBLE, NEW INTERNATIONAL VERSION®. NIV®. Copyright © 1973, 1978, 1984 by International Bible Society. Used by permission of Zondervan Publishing House. All rights reserved.

The "NIV" and "New International Version" trademarks are registered in the United States Patent and Trademark Office by International Bible Society. Use of either trademark requires the permission of International Bible Society.

All rights reserved. No part of this publication may be reproduced, stored in a retrieval system, or transmitted in any form or by any means—electronic, mechanical, photocopy, recording, or otherwise—except for brief quotations in reviews, without prior permission from the publisher.

Library of Congress Card 93-84930
Northwestern Publishing House
1250 N. 113th St., Milwaukee, WI 53226-3284
© 1993 by Northwestern Publishing House.
Published 1993
Printed in the United States of America
ISBN 978-0-8100-0500-6
ISBN 978-0-8100-2925-5 (e-book)

Contents

1. We Are Not Our Own 5
2. Come and See 8
3. More Precious than Gold 11
4. Children of Light 14
5. Precious Savior 17
6. Things Above 20
7. The Book 23
8. Follow Jesus 27
9. That We Might Live 30
10. The Bitter Made Sweet 34
11. Behold the Lamb of God 38
12. Precious Promises 42
13. Behind His Back 46
14. A Conference with God 49
15. God Hears Us 53
16. O Lord! How Long? 57
17. Acceptable Prayer 60
18. Praise His Holy Name 65
19. Our Ministering Angels 68

20. Die, Yet Live	72
21. Our Redemption	76
22. Salvation Is Free	80
23. The Open Heaven	83
24. Headed for Glory	87
25. Forgetting Can Be Good	91
26. Profitable Affliction	94
27. Beneficial Warning	97
28. Let Us Use Our Gifts	101
29. Serving with Gladness	104
30. A More Convenient Season	108
31. The Truth	111
32. Make the Devil Flee	114
33. A Haunted House	117
34. Hold Fast	121
35. Personal Responsibility	125
36. As Long as It Is Day	128
37. The Final Victory	131

1.

We Are Not Our Own

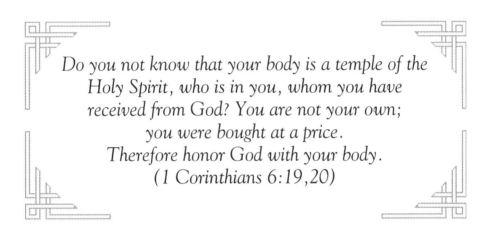

Do you not know that your body is a temple of the Holy Spirit, who is in you, whom you have received from God? You are not your own; you were bought at a price. Therefore honor God with your body.
(1 Corinthians 6:19,20)

We are not our own. What a complete contradiction to the popular idea that the vast majority of people in our day have about themselves! They live and conduct themselves according to the belief that they are their own person and have every right to do as they please and are not responsible to anyone else. For them the very thought that they should belong to another and be guided and directed by another is completely foreign and does not make any sense. But the fact remains, that is exactly what the Scriptures tell us. We are not our own. We belong to God and are responsible to him.

We are his first of all by right of creation and preservation. "Know that the LORD is God. It is he who made us, and we are his" (Psalm 100:3). And as he has given us life, so he also sustains it by his divine providence. "The eyes of all look to you, and you give them their food at the proper time. You open your hand and satisfy the desires of every living thing" (Psalm 145:15,16). In this way all mankind belongs to God and comes under his care and keeping.

Both the Corinthian Christians and all the rest of us who believe in the triune God are also his own by reason of redemption. We were bought with a price. And what a price it was! Not with gold or silver or other treasures of earth, but with the holy, precious blood and innocent, bitter suffering and death of the only-begotten Son of God was the ransom paid for the sins of the world. Paid for all and freely offered in the gospel, it becomes the possession of all who accept it by faith and thereby acknowledge God as their Lord.

Our obligation for this tremendous sacrifice is plainly and simply stated: Therefore glorify God. Not just an external superficial expression of praise is called for here, but glorifying God in our bodies and in our spirits. God has given us our bodies as a trust, and he wants us to use them accordingly. We have no right to abuse and ruin them. They are the temples of the Holy Spirit and as such deserve to be treated with proper respect and care.

God has given us varying bodily gifts with which we can glorify him. With some it may be good physical strength and endurance as well as diligence to serve him by being faithful in their chosen calling. Others may have received special talents and skills to employ in his name in building his kingdom. We can glorify God by sharing our time and gifts with the less fortunate out of love for them and the Lord. Such deeds of love Jesus promises to recognize in the Last Judgment. "The King will reply, 'I tell you the truth, whatever you did for one of the least of these brothers of mine, you did for me'" (Matthew 25:40).

In this task of glorifying God the body works together with the mind and spirit that give direction to the body. Experience and education help to enrich our life of giving glory to God.

> All glory be to God alone,
> Forevermore the Highest One,
> Who doth our sinful race befriend
> And grace and peace to us extend.
> Among mankind may His good will
> All hearts with deep thanksgiving fill.
>
> We praise Thee, God, and Thee we bless;
> We worship Thee in humbleness;
> From day to day we glorify
> Thee, everlasting God on high.
> Of Thy great glory do we sing,
> And e'er to Thee our thanks we bring.
>
> Amen, this ever true shall be,
> As angels sing adoringly.
> By all creation, far and wide,
> Thou, Lord, art ever glorified;
> And Thee all Christendom doth praise
> Now and through everlasting days.
> (TLH 238:1,2,6)

Come and See

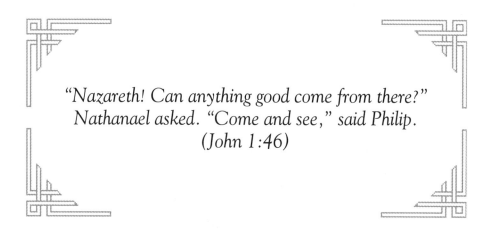

"Nazareth! Can anything good come from there?" Nathanael asked. "Come and see," said Philip. (John 1:46)

In the narrative from which these words are taken we see how Nathanael was won for Jesus. His friend Philip had just been chosen by Jesus to become one of his apostles. Full of excitement and enthusiasm, his first thought was to share his joy with Nathanael. "We have found the one Moses wrote about in the Law," he declares, "and about whom the prophets also wrote—Jesus of Nazareth, the son of Joseph" (John 1:45). "We have found the promised Messiah," Philip was telling Nathanael.

Nathanael's response is more restrained. He hesitates as he weighs the enthusiastic message of his friend.

Obscure little Nazareth? Can that be? "Can anything good come from there?"

Philip does not attempt to argue. He wisely replies, "Come and see." He is sure that Jesus can do much better at convincing Nathanael than he can.

Nathanael kept an open mind and an open heart and accepted the challenge of his friend to see for himself whether Jesus of Nazareth was all that Philip had said of him. Any doubts that he still had were quickly swept away when Jesus demonstrated his omniscience to him.

Even as Nathanael approached, Jesus identified him as a true and sincere Israelite who was waiting for the fulfillment of the Messianic prophecies. Taken by surprise at this display of knowledge about him, Nathanael was even more overwhelmed when Jesus told him that he saw him under the fig tree before Philip had invited him to come and see.

We are not told what Nathanael was doing under the fig tree, but there is just a hint that he was engaged in meditation and prayer where he was alone with God. Unlike the hypocrites, who liked to pray on the street corners and in the market places where they could be admired of men, there was no guile, "nothing false," in this "true Israelite."

In Nathanael's estimation, he had witnessed a miracle, and he was completely won for Jesus. He confessed then and there, "Rabbi, you are the Son of God; you are the King of Israel" (John 1:49).

"Come and see" is all that God asks of anyone who has doubts about the person or work of Jesus. And while it is not possible in our day to meet him physically and to observe him personally as Nathanael was able to do, we can see his presence in the Bible, where he has clearly revealed himself. If we will search the Scriptures with an open heart and mind, he will manifest his divinity in a way that we will readily recognize.

Come and see, and you will find the Friend of sinners, who loves them deeply and is ready to forgive the penitent and remove the barrier that separates them from the holy God.

Come and see, and behold a compassionate and understanding Helper who does not hesitate to touch the unclean as he administers his healing power.

Come and see that he will give rest to the weary, strength to the weak, and peace to the troubled and oppressed who give heed to his gracious invitation.

Come and see that something good has indeed come out of Nazareth: the Son of God and the Savior of the world, who has conquered death and the powers of darkness and has risen triumphantly from the grave. And because he lives we shall live also.

> The Savior calls; let ev'ry ear
> Attend the heav'nly sound.
> Ye doubting souls, dismiss your fear;
> Hope smiles reviving round.
>
> Ye sinners, come, 'tis Mercy's voice;
> The gracious call obey;
> Mercy invites to heav'nly joys,
> And can you yet delay?

(TLH 281:1,4)

More Precious than Gold

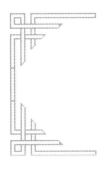
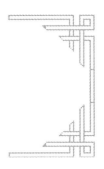

*They are more precious than gold,
than much pure gold.
(Psalm 19:10)*

Gold! Gold! Gold!
Bright and yellow, hard and cold,
Molten, graven, hammered and rolled,
Heavy to get and light to hold!
Hoarded, bartered, bought and sold,
Stolen, borrowed, squandered, doled,
Spurned by the young, but hugged by the old
To the very verge of the churchyard mould;
Price of many a crime untold—
Gold! Gold! Gold!

—Thomas Hood

Gold and its companion, money, are the most universally desired and ardently sought after objects on this earth. The passion to acquire and accumulate them is present everywhere among mankind, and it drives people on to enormous efforts and extreme sacrifices.

The psalmist knows something much more precious and therefore more to be desired. It is the precious Word of God, a treasure far surpassing the most fabulous riches of earth.

No amount of shining gold can buy admission into the mansions of God in heaven, but the saving Word of God is able to convert the soul from sin and unbelief to faith and trust in God and to open the gates of Paradise.

Money cannot purchase divine wisdom, but the sacred Scripture is able to make even the simple wise and to teach them to see and follow the way that leads to eternal life.

Earthly wealth may give joy to the heart for a time, but it can give no assurance of permanent joy and happiness. On the contrary, it frequently produces its own cares and worries. God's Word, on the other hand, invites us to cast all our anxieties and burdens on the Lord, with the assurance that he will care for us (1 Peter 5:7).

Gold is indeed noted for its lasting beauty. It will not rust like iron nor tarnish like silver. It is not subject to deterioration or decay. But it can never compare in permanence with the abiding Word of the eternal God. Jesus says: "I tell you the truth. . . . Heaven and earth will pass away, but my words will never pass away" (Matthew 24:34,35).

No amount of money can buy the forgiveness of sins and peace of conscience, but the Word of God offers both as a free gift of the heavenly Father. It is foolish—

even worse—it is fatal to permit the glitter of gold to lure us into making material possessions our highest goal in life. They cannot truly satisfy the longing of the soul for fellowship with God. All the wealth of earth is not enough to redeem one soul, as Jesus puts it: "What good will it be for a man if he gains the whole world, yet forfeits his soul? Or what can a man give in exchange for his soul?" (Matthew 16:26)

Life and salvation are freely proclaimed and given through the living Word, truly making it more to be desired than gold, than much fine gold.

> Speak, O Lord, Thy servant heareth,
> To Thy Word I now give heed;
> Life and spirit Thy Word beareth,
> All Thy Word is true indeed.
> Death's dread pow'r in me is rife;
> Jesus, may Thy Word of Life
> Fill my soul with love's strong fervor
> That I cling to Thee forever.
>
> Lord, Thy words are waters living
> Where I quench my thirsty need;
> Lord, Thy words are bread life-giving,
> On Thy words my soul doth feed.
> Lord, Thy words shall be my light
> Through death's vale and dreary night;
> Yea, they are my sword prevailing
> And my cup of joy unfailing.
>
> (TLH 296:1,3)

4.

Children of Light

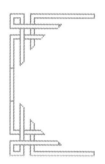
*For you were once darkness,
but now you are light in the Lord.
Live as children of light.*
(Ephesians 5:8)
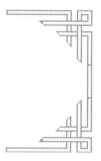

Children of light is one of the most notable titles given to Christians in the Bible. It describes the high esteem which they enjoy in the kingdom of God as well as the heavy responsibility that is placed upon them. By nature they were all in the darkness of sin and unbelief, even as the Ephesian Christians had been before they were rescued by the light of the gospel and made children of light.

What a wonderful thing light is! It was the first gift of God to the newly created world and its inhabitants. Gloom and darkness were driven away, and life prospered on the illuminated earth.

Darkness cannot illuminate itself. Light must be brought in from another source to replace the darkness. This applies in the spiritual realm as well as in the natural or physical realm. Light and darkness stand in direct contrast to each other. Spiritual darkness represents sin, evil, ignorance, decay, and death. Spiritual light, on the other hand, represents goodness, purity, strength, knowledge, truth, life, and joy. Its source is in God, for "God is light; in him there is no darkness at all" (1 John 1:5).

The children of light are those who have been called out of the darkness of sin and unbelief by Christ and made God's own through the gracious work of the Holy Spirit. As citizens of the kingdom of light they are pilgrims on the earth. Their native land is heaven (cp. Philippians 3:20).

Let us never lose sight of who we are, even as Paul reminded the Thessalonian Christians: "You are all sons of the light and sons of the day. We do not belong to the night or to the darkness" (1 Thessalonians 5:5).

Along with the high privilege and honor of being children of God and children of light and having fellowship with God comes the corresponding duty and responsibility to "live as children of light." We have the duty to let our light shine by leading a life that is pleasing to God. Our deeds as well as our words are to show clearly and unmistakably that we are children of light. Our highest calling is to be a light that lights the way to eternal life for those who are still sitting in darkness. Walking in darkness is failing in our God-given duty and denies fellowship with God. Yielding to the temptations of the prince of darkness is disastrous. It separates from God and leads to eternal death.

Walking in the light is not wandering to and fro or searching right and left for the enticements that the world has to offer. Rather, it is traveling with a firm and sure step to the source and fountain of light, guided by its shining beams to light the way. Facing the goal as we steadfastly march forward, the shadows of sin will be cast behind us as we are welcomed by our forgiving Lord.

With Israel of old we share the gracious invitation: "Come, O house of Jacob, let us walk in the light of the LORD" (Isaiah 2:5).

> Renew me, O eternal Light,
> And let my heart and soul be bright,
> Illumined with the light of grace
> That issues from Thy holy face.
>
> Destroy in me the lust of sin,
> From all impureness make me clean.
> Oh, grant me pow'r and strength, my God,
> To strive against my flesh and blood!
>
> (TLH 398:1,2)

Precious Savior

For in Scripture it says: "See, I lay a stone in Zion, a chosen and precious cornerstone, and the one who trusts in him will never be put to shame."
(1 Peter 2:6)

> O Savior, precious Savior,
> Whom, yet unseen, we love;
> O name of might and favor,
> All other names above,
> We worship Thee, we bless Thee,
> To Thee, O Christ, we sing;
> We praise Thee and confess Thee,
> Our holy Lord and King.
>
> (TLH 352:1)

More precious by far than sparkling gems and shining jewels and all the other admired treasures of earth is the priceless gift of the heavenly Father, our precious Lord and Savior, Jesus Christ.

The apostle Peter observes that for many people Jesus Christ became a stumbling block and rock of offense instead of the chief cornerstone and firm foundation on which his church is built, even as Isaiah had foretold. For those who believe, however, Peter declares him to be precious.

Indeed, though Jesus, a living stone, was despised and rejected by many, he was chosen by God and precious to him (1 Peter 2:4). Therefore we also esteem him most highly and count him dear and precious to us.

God himself gave him a precious name when he directed Joseph in a dream: "You are to give him the name Jesus [Savior], because he will save his people from their sins" (Matthew 1:21). And standing before the Council, Peter declares, "Rulers and elders of the people! . . . He is 'the stone you builders rejected, which has become the capstone.' Salvation is found in no one else, for there is no other name under heaven given to men by which we must be saved" (Acts 4:8,11,12).

Corresponding to his precious name are his precious works and teachings. Answering John the Baptist's question about himself, Jesus said: "Go back and report to John what you hear and see: The blind receive sight, the lame walk, those who have leprosy are cured, the deaf hear, the dead are raised, and the good news is preached to the poor" (Matthew 11:4,5). At the transfiguration the heavenly Father's approval came in these words: "This is my Son, whom I love; with him I am well pleased. Listen to him!" (Matthew 17:5). This approval was reinforced by raising Jesus from the dead and exalting him to his own right hand of majesty and power.

How marvelous that this precious Savior should love us sinful and disobedient human beings enough to offer himself as our substitute and to shed his precious blood for our redemption! The apostle emphasizes the tremendous price that was paid. "For you know that it was not with perishable things such as silver or gold that you were redeemed . . . but with the precious blood of Christ" (1 Peter 1:18,19).

No wonder the heavenly host is portrayed in the vision of John as singing in celebration: "You were slain, and with your blood you purchased men for God" (Revelation 5:9).

> Thou, O Christ, art all I want;
> More than all in Thee I find.
> Raise the fallen, cheer the faint,
> Heal the sick, and lead the blind.
> Just and holy is Thy name;
> I am all unrighteousness,
> False and full of sin I am;
> Thou art full of truth and grace.
>
> (TLH 345:4)

6.

Things Above

*Set your minds on things above,
not on earthly things.
(Colossians 3:2)*

True Christians, whose lives have been renewed by the Savior's sacrificial death and resurrection, are exhorted to reflect that change in their daily living. This means keeping the priorities straight and placing the *things above* ahead of the things on earth, not only in our thinking, but particularly also in our way of life. God's Word says: "So then, just as you received Christ Jesus as Lord, continue to live in him" (Colossians 2:6).

The "earthly things" consist of a variety of kinds or classes. Among them are the kinds of things that were prevalent among the Colossians in their former life style.

They included immorality, greed, covetousness, selfishness, anger, malice, lying, insults, as well as other sins and vices. These are to be put off and shunned. Less flagrant, but also evil in their effect, are the worries and cares into which we can so easily become immersed. Striving to the utmost for praise and honor to feed our pride and vanity poses grave danger for the soul. The same is true of the desire to hoard great wealth or other treasures.

Our gracious heavenly Father, out of his boundless love, has placed many wonderful and beautiful things upon the earth for our benefit and enjoyment. "Every good and perfect gift is from above, coming down from the Father of the heavenly lights" (James 1:17). To spurn these blessings would be gross ingratitude, and Scripture summons us: "Praise the LORD, O my soul, and forget not all his benefits" (Psalm 103:2).

God does not call on Christians to hate the world, which he has made. He expects us to appreciate the blessings of health and home and family and others more. But even those things which are beautiful and good and noble in themselves dare not be allowed to absorb our total interest or to become our highest concern in life. They dare not distract our minds from the things above. "For this world in its present form is passing away" (1 Corinthians 7:31). Only the things above will remain into eternity.

We need to remember that "here we do not have an enduring city, but we are looking for the city that is to come" (Hebrews 13:14). That is why we are so earnestly exhorted to aspire to the realms above where Christ, our victorious Lord and Savior, is sitting at the right hand of the Father with power and authority. Look up to him! Look heavenward where he has gone to prepare a place of indescribable beauty and delight for us. Set your affections on things above and eagerly look forward to seeing our beloved Savior face-to-face and to living with him in perfect peace and harmony.

In the higher realm of heaven there will be no infirmities of the body to trouble us, no pain or tears, no sin or temptation to mar the perfect bliss. There all shall have glorified bodies similar to the glorious body of Jesus, which his chosen disciples were privileged to preview on the Mount of Transfiguration (Matthew 17:2).

As a redeemed child of God who believes in Jesus as your Savior, your name has been written in heaven in the Book of Life. Let your thoughts rise often to the things above while you wait for the Lord's summon to enter into your inheritance in Paradise.

> Grant that I only Thee may love
> And seek those things which are above
> Till I behold Thee face to face,
> O Light eternal, through Thy grace.

* * *

> O sweet and blessed country,
> The home of God's elect!
> O sweet and blessed country
> That eager hearts expect!
> Jesus, in mercy bring us
> To that dear land of rest,
> Who art, with God the Father
> And Spirit, ever blest.

(TLH 398:4; 613:4)

7.

The Book

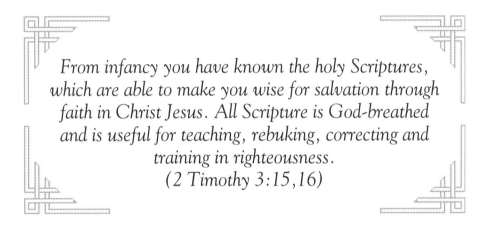

From infancy you have known the holy Scriptures, which are able to make you wise for salvation through faith in Christ Jesus. All Scripture is God-breathed and is useful for teaching, rebuking, correcting and training in righteousness.
(2 Timothy 3:15,16)

    The commonly accepted and used name for the Holy Scriptures or the Word of God is "The Bible." This name is derived from the Greek word "biblion," meaning book. Countless books have been written over the years. King Solomon already stated in his day, "Of making many books there is no end" (Ecclesiastes 12:12). Many of these, however, can only be called a book. Only the Holy Scriptures deserves to be called THE BOOK.

    THE BOOK is totally unique in its origin. Though written by men over a period of many centuries, it was inspired by God and is therefore his own divine Word.

Speaking through the apostle Paul to Timothy in the word under consideration, God declares: "All Scripture is God-breathed." Through Peter he explains: "Men spoke from God as they were carried along by the Holy Spirit" (2 Peter 1:21). St. Paul commends the Thessalonian Christians: "When you received the word of God, which you heard from us, you accepted it not as the word of men, but as it actually is, the word of God" (1 Thessalonians 2:13). God indeed claims THE BOOK as his own, and already in the Old Testament he declares: "Let the one who has my word speak it faithfully" (Jeremiah 23:28).

THE BOOK brings a message from the throne of God in heaven. It is a timeless message, as true and fitting today as it was in the day of the patriarchs and of the apostles, and it will continue to be so until time merges with eternity. "Heaven and earth will pass away, but my words will never pass away" (Matthew 24:35). In it God reveals himself as the Savior of sinners. He speaks to us of his boundless love, by which he offers full pardon and forgiveness for the sake of Jesus' perfect sacrifice to all who repent of their sins.

THE BOOK extends a most gracious invitation: "Come to me, all you who are weary and burdened, and I will give you rest" (Matthew 11:28). To this is added the promise, "Whoever comes to me I will never drive away" (John 6:37).

THE BOOK is for all people, whatever their circumstances or station in life, and whatever their age or occupation may be. It is for people of all nationalities and races and languages.

In the Book of Books God comes personally to those who will listen and pay attention. The message it brings is reliable and trustworthy because it is not the word of men but the inspired Word of God. THE BOOK does not merely contain the Word of God; it is his Word from cover to cover. It answers the age-old question: "What must I do to be saved?" (Acts 16:30). It responds: "Believe in the Lord Jesus, and you will be saved—you and your household" (Acts 16:31).

THE BOOK tells us all that we need to know for our salvation. There is nothing missing; nothing is to be added to guide us on the way to eternal life. It is not the case of THE BOOK plus some other revelation, rule, or guide. It is the sole authority in matters of faith and life. We should not listen to "pied pipers" who would try to lead us astray.

Let us prize THE BOOK above everything and use it diligently and faithfully. Let us heed the voice of Jesus: "You diligently study the Scriptures because you think that by them you possess eternal life. These are the Scriptures that testify about me" (John 5:39).

> How precious is the Book Divine,
> By inspiration giv'n!
> Bright as a lamp its doctrines shine
> To guide our souls to heav'n.
>
> Its light, descending from above
> Our gloomy world to cheer,
> Displays a Savior's boundless love
> And brings his glories near.

It shows to man his wand'ring ways
And where his feet have trod,
And brings to view the matchless grace
Of a forgiving God.

It sweetly cheers our drooping hearts
In this dark vale of tears.
Life, light, and joy it still imparts
And quells our rising fears.

This lamp through all the tedious night
Of life shall guide our way
Till we behold the clearer light
Of an eternal day.

(TLH 285:1-3,5,6)

8.

Follow Jesus

[Jesus] said: "If anyone would come after me, he must deny himself and take up his cross and follow me."
(Mark 8:34)

The name Jesus was quite common among the Jews. It means "the Lord is salvation." The name gained special meaning when it was divinely chosen as the human name for the Son of God to indicate his purpose for coming to earth: to save his people from their sins.

To fulfill this mission he gathered followers to lead and to train. The first among them were Andrew and John, followers of John the Baptist. They responded to John's witness of Jesus as the Lamb of God by becoming followers of Jesus. They then found their brothers and brought them to Jesus. Others heeded the direct summons of Jesus, as did Levi, the tax collector at Capernaum. When Jesus told him, "Follow me," he left all and followed and marked his new life with the new name, Matthew, which means Gift of God.

For a time Jesus was very popular. The people were spellbound by his vigorous teaching and his amazing miracles; consequently, they flocked to him by the thousands. When he fed the multitude with the loaves and fishes, their admiration and enthusiasm grew, and they wanted to make him their king. But when he did not want to be their earthly king, many were disappointed and turned their backs on him.

These people were not interested in him as the Messiah, the promised Savior from sin; rather, they sought him as a man who could supply their earthly wants. Their desertions thinned the ranks of his followers.

There were also defections among the disciples (John 6:66). Former soldiers of the cross, they found his teaching a hard saying, and they "turned back and no longer followed him."

To follow Jesus is not, nor ever has been, an easy, half-way measure. It is a challenge to be active in his service. It means to be ready to put aside our personal self-interest and become his disciples and have him lead. It means to listen to him when he speaks to us in his divine Word and to obey him. It means trusting him to guide us on the right way, even when that way is contrary to our desires and inclinations. It means bearing the cross of affliction and hardships.

Come, follow Me, the Savior spake,
All in My way abiding;
Deny yourselves, the world forsake,
Obey My call and guiding.
Oh, bear the cross, whate'er betide,
Take My example for your guide.

(TLH 421:1)

Following Jesus "at a distance," as Peter did on that memorable night, is not the kind of following that Jesus wants. It does not show him the honor and devotion he deserves. It is also dangerous for the follower. It is a sign that loyalty to the Master is weakening, and the danger of falling away from him completely is very real.

It is not enough to have been a follower of Jesus for a time. Those who neglect or ignore the salvation Jesus won will not escape God's judgment. Whoever is a loyal and faithful follower to the end has God's promise of the crown of eternal life.

Jesus, lead Thou on
Till our rest is won;
And although the way be cheerless,
We will follow calm and fearless.
Guide us by Thy hand
To our fatherland.

Jesus, lead Thou on
Till our rest is won.
Heav'nly Leader, still direct us,
Still support, control, protect us,
Till we safely stand
In our fatherland.

(TLH 410:1,4)

9.

That We Might Live

*This is how God showed his love among us:
He sent his one and only Son into the world
that we might live through him.
(1 John 4:9)*

Love is a very familiar word. We hear it and see it used everywhere. In our language it has a very wide range of usage and meaning, from sentimental liking and selfish desire to deep affection, noble concern, and exalted self-sacrifice. The language in which the New Testament was written is much more precise. In it different words are use to describe different kinds of love.

When the Bible tells us that "God is love" (1 John 4:8), it speaks of the noblest and most exalted form of love and ascribes it to his very essence and nature. This perfect love streams forth from his overflowing heart to carry his blessings far and wide.

The God of love has countless ways to exhibit his divine love and bestow his blessings. He surrounds us with the beauty of his creation—land and sea, clouds and sunshine, the beauty of flowers and the song of birds. He provides us with food and shelter for our bodily needs and much more. He brings joy and peace and contentment into the lives of those who welcome him. Wherever we look we see the evidence of his marvelous love.

But God showed his love in the highest way when he sent his only Son into the world that we might live through him. By comparison with all other examples of his divine love, this stands out as the very ultimate. Nothing greater than this is possible.

And the amazing thing is that this boundless love was so freely given without finding any special quality or attractiveness in us. On the contrary, since the fall of man into sin all mankind is by nature opposed to the will of God and prone to vice, and "every inclination of his heart is evil from childhood" (Genesis 8:21). "All have turned aside, they have together become corrupt; there is no one who does good, not even one" (Psalm 14:3). There is no distinction "for all have sinned and fall short of the glory of God" (Romans 3:23).

God loved us because love is his very nature. Love compelled him to pay the uttermost price. "He who did not spare his own Son, but gave him up for us all" (Romans 8:32).

His love was an all-embracing love. No one is excluded. "For God so loved the world that he gave his one and only Son, that whoever believes in him shall not perish but have eternal life" (John 3:16).

The Father's amazing love was fully matched by the love of his only-begotten Son, Jesus Christ, who was totally committed to doing the Father's will. He showed his love in his concern for all kinds of people, the poor and the common people as well as those of rank and position. His heart went out in sympathy and compassion to those in special need: the lepers, the blind, the sick, and the widows. He had a special love for little children. His gracious invitation still stands: "Come to me, all you who are weary and burdened, and I will give you rest" (Matthew 11:28).

The miracle of God's love is that he loved us when we were so unloving and unlovely. "This is love: not that we loved God, but that he loved us" (1 John 4:10). Our love to God is in response to his surpassing love for us by which we obtain the assurance of eternal life. Now he wants us to respond to that love by showing love to others. "Dear friends, since God so loved us, we also ought to love one another" (1 John 4:11). Then divine love becomes the motive and drive for brotherly love, causing it to blossom and bear fruit also in this life.

> Thine forever, God of Love!
> Hear us from Thy throne above,
> Thine forever may we be
> Here and in eternity!
>
> Thine forever! Thou our Guide,
> All our wants by Thee supplied,
> All our sins by Thee forgiven;
> Lead us, Lord, from earth to heaven.

* * *

Eternal Triune Lord,
Let all the hosts above,
Let all the sons of men record,
And dwell upon, Thy love.

(TLH 338:1,5; 241:4)

10.

The Bitter Made Sweet

> *When they came to Marah, they could not drink its water because it was bitter. (That is why the place is called Marah.) So the people grumbled against Moses, saying, "What are we to drink?" Then Moses cried out to the* LORD, *and the* LORD *showed him a piece of wood. He threw it into the water, and the water became sweet.*
> (Exodus 15:23-25)

An incident of bygone years that still fascinates God's people is the sweetening of the bitter waters of Marah. Its warm appeal, which captivates the imagination of the Christian, is no doubt due to the parallel between his own experience and that of Israel.

Three days earlier the Israelites were in high spirits. At last they were free and safe. Their slavery in Egypt was over. God had forced the oppressors to let Israel go. When it had seemed that the venture might fail before it got well under way, God had come to the rescue of his people and had led them dry-shod through the Red Sea and caused Pharaoh's pursuing army to be destroyed. Their hearts overflowed with songs of exuberant joy and thanksgiving.

But how quickly things can change! After only three short days the voice of singing was no longer heard. In its place had come grumbling and complaining which flowed from bitter and discontented hearts. The first lap of the journey from the Red Sea was a forty-mile march into the wilderness of Shur. The vast host traveled slowly through the parched and barren region. By the time they came to the waters of Marah both man and beast were suffering from thirst. Eagerly they rushed forward to quench their burning thirst, but when they tasted the water they found it was bitter and unfit to drink. Disappointment gave way to complaint. Bitterly they challenged Moses, "What are we to drink?"

Moses did what the people in their rebellion and unbelief had failed to do. He went to the throne of the gracious God and pleaded the people's cause. God commanded him to put a certain tree into the water, whereupon it lost its bitterness and became sweet and palatable, and the people could quench their thirst.

It was necessary for Israel to learn how dependent they really were on the power and help of God. Without him they were utterly helpless and would never reach the Promised Land. Only with his help could they succeed.

Israel's journey from the house of bondage in Egypt to the land of promise in Canaan reminds us of our pilgrimage through life, that is, from our bondage of sin and Satan to our entry into the heavenly Canaan. On this pilgrimage we meet with experiences that fill our mouths with thanksgiving and praise. At other times they are sad and discouraging. We are led figuratively to Marah's brink, where our parched and weary body finds only water that is bitter and unpalatable. In our distress we cry to the Lord, and he hears our prayer. Mercifully he extracts the bitterness from our woes and makes the evil serve our good. Then we learn "that in all things God works for the good of those who love him" (Romans 8:28).

The children of God have joy and hope amid sorrow and affliction. The losses of life cannot take the peace of God out of their hearts. They know that it is part of God's plan for them to enter the kingdom of God through many hardships. But God also shows his marvelous love and grace by removing the bitterness from those hardships. As the wretchedness and distress recede, the kingdom of God and the mansions of the Father's house, which Christ prepared for us by means of his perfect obedience and his sacrificial death, fill our horizon. Then the child of God can exclaim with the apostle: "I consider that our present sufferings are not worth comparing with the glory that will be revealed in us" (Romans 8:18).

> Savior, I follow on, guided by Thee,
> Seeing not yet the hand that leadeth me.
> Hushed be my heart and still, fear I no further ill,
> Only to meet Thy will my will shall be.
>
> Riven the rock for me Thirst to relieve,
> Manna from heaven falls fresh ev'ry eve.

Never a want severe causeth my eye a tear
But Thou dost whisper near, "Only believe."

Often to Marah's brink have I been brought;
Shrinking the cup to drink, help I have sought;
And with the prayer's ascent
     Jesus the branch hath rent,
Quickly relief hath sent, sweet'ning the draught.

                               (TLH 422:1-3)

Behold the Lamb of God

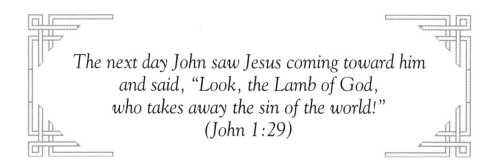

The next day John saw Jesus coming toward him and said, "Look, the Lamb of God, who takes away the sin of the world!"
(John 1:29)

For almost thirty-five centuries the greatest annual celebration of the Jews has been the Passover Festival to commemorate their deliverance from the bondage of Egypt and the birthright of their nation. Today the main feature of the Jewish Passover observance is the family worship, or seder, around the festive table with the singing of psalms, the rehearsal of the deliverance, the prayers, and the traditional Passover meal. Near the end of the seder the small children arise from the table to open the front door of the house for Elijah, the prophet. The hope of every Jewish family is that on Passover Elijah will come to herald the Messiah, the Son of David, who will gather them all home to the land of Israel. When Elijah does not appear, they expectantly look forward to next year.

The tragic part of this meaningful observance is the failure to realize and understand that "Elijah" made his expected appearance already long ago and announced the coming of the Messiah when he proclaimed Jesus of Nazareth as the Lamb of God.

The promise of Elijah's coming to prepare the way for the Messiah went back four hundred years to Malachi, the last of the Old Testament prophets. He wrote: "See, I will send my messenger, who will prepare the way before me. Then suddenly the Lord you are seeking will come to his temple. . . . See, I will send you the prophet Elijah before that great and dreadful day of the LORD comes. He will turn the hearts of the fathers to their children, and the hearts of the children to their fathers; or else I will come and strike the land with a curse" (Malachi 3:1; 4:5,6).

There can be no question about this prophecy being fulfilled in John the Baptist. At the announcement of his impending birth the angel Gabriel said to Zechariah, his father: "He will be great in the sight of the Lord . . . and he will be filled with the Holy Spirit even from birth. Many of the people of Israel will he bring back to the Lord their God. And he will go on before the Lord, in the spirit and power of Elijah, to turn the hearts of the fathers to their children and the disobedient to the wisdom of the righteous—to make ready a people prepared for the Lord" (Luke 1:15-17). After John's birth, Zechariah, full of the Spirit, prophesied in his Benedictus: "And you, my child, will be called a prophet of the Most High; for you will go on before the Lord to prepare the way for him, to give his people the knowledge of salvation through the forgiveness of their sins" (Luke 1:76,77).

To this we add the witness of Jesus: "This is the one about whom it is written: 'I will send my messenger ahead of you, who will prepare your way before you.' . . . For all the Prophets and the Law prophesied until John. And if you are willing to accept it, he is the Elijah who was to come" (Matthew 11:10,13,14).

John the Baptist faithfully fulfilled his divinely chosen calling by preaching repentance to the people and by directing them to Jesus, the Lamb that God himself provided as a sacrifice for the sins of the world. The sacrifice was made on Calvary's cross and is complete.

> When all the world was cursed
> By Moses' condemnation,
> Saint John the Baptist came
> With words of consolation.
> With true forerunner's zeal
> The Greater One he named,
> And Him, as yet unknown,
> As Savior he proclaimed.
>
> Behold the Lamb of God
> That bears the world's transgression,
> Whose sacrifice removes
> The Enemy's oppression.
> Behold the Lamb of God,
> Who beareth all our sin,
> Who for our peace and joy
> Will full atonement win.

Thrice blessed every one
Who heeds the proclamation
Which John the Baptist brought,
Accepting Christ's salvation.
He who believes this truth
And comes with love unfeigned
Has righteousness and peace
In fullest measure gained.

                (TLH 272:1,3,4)

Precious Promises

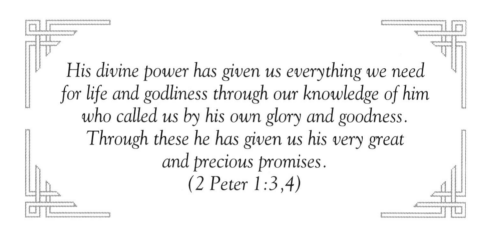

His divine power has given us everything we need for life and godliness through our knowledge of him who called us by his own glory and goodness. Through these he has given us his very great and precious promises.
(2 Peter 1:3,4)

Promises made and kept constitute a very significant part of a meaningful and satisfying life here on earth. Our relationships with others, whether in business, on the job, in the family, in the church, or in the community, depend in a large measure on how reliable our promises to one another are.

Even more significant to us are the promises which govern our relationship with God—his promises to us and ours to him.

The Bible is full of promises from the beginning to the end. Someone has counted more than thirty-two thousand of them. Their range is as wide as the needs and the blessings of humankind.

Sometimes these promises pertain to individual persons as in the case of Jacob. When he was compelled to flee from the wrath of his brother Esau, he was given the promise of God's protective presence. "I am with you and will watch over you wherever you go, and I will bring you back to this land. I will not leave you until I have done what I have promised you" (Genesis 28:15).

At other times God's promises encompass the whole human race. After Adam and Eve had forfeited Paradise through sinful pride and disobedience, God graciously promised a Savior from sin, a promise repeated many times until fulfilled with the birth of Christ at Bethlehem. The weary and burdened are invited by Jesus to come unto him, and he promises to give them rest. Those who are troubled and fearful are promised peace. Those caught in the bondage of sin are promised deliverance, and those entrapped by error shall be made free. Jesus says: "If you hold to my teaching, you are really my disciples. Then you will know the truth, and the truth will set you free" (John 8:31,32). He promises that his words shall endure: "Heaven and earth will pass away, but my words will never pass away" (Matthew 24:35). God promises to support us: "Cast your cares on the LORD and he will sustain you" (Psalm 55:22). Like Asaph, who trusted the guidance of God's counsel, we, too, have God's promise to receive us into glory with him (cp. Psalm 73:24).

This is but a small sample of the great and marvelous promises which God has made in his Word; they reflect his fatherly care and concern for us. There is no reason for us to doubt or question them. They are not to be compared to the promises of weak and fickle men who are prone to forget and often promise more than they are able or even intend to keep. "God is not a man, that he should lie" (Number 23:19). He does not change like the shifting shadows. He is the almighty God who tells us: "I the LORD do not change" (Malachi 3:6). His promises are trustworthy and dependable. "For no matter how many promises God has made, they are 'Yes' in Christ. And so through him the 'Amen' is spoken by us to the glory of God" (2 Corinthians 1:20). Through God's precious and very great promises our lives are wonderfully blessed and enriched.

Alas, our promises to God are not as sure and firmly kept as his are to us. The love of many who pledged lifelong loyalty before his altar has grown cold, and they have drifted away. All of us are besieged by the enticements of the world and our own sinful nature, so that we are in constant danger of breaking our promises. We must continually be on our guard. Even the strongest and most confident disciples can fall in the hour of temptation if they rely on their own strength as Peter did. How precious, then, the promise that when we do stumble and fall we will not be rejected, but pardoned and restored when we repent and seek forgiveness!

> Let each day begin with prayer,
> Praise, and adoration;
> On the Lord cast ev'ry care,
> He is thy Salvation.
> Morning, evening, and at night
> Jesus will be near thee,

Save thee from the Tempter's might,
With His presence cheer thee.

With thy Savior at thy side,
Foes need not alarm thee;
In His promises confide,
And no ill can harm thee.
All thy trust do thou repose
In the mighty Master,
Who in wisdom truly knows
How to stem disaster.

(TLH 540:2,3)

13.

Behind His Back

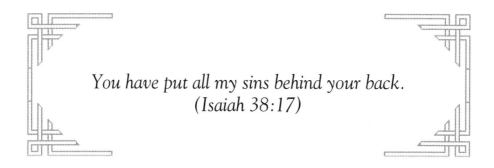

You have put all my sins behind your back.
(Isaiah 38:17)

In the Apostles' Creed we confess with all Christendom, "I believe in the forgiveness of sins." This central doctrine of our faith rests firmly upon the Scriptures of both the Old and the New Testaments. It presents the foremost and absolute need of the sinner, forgiveness of sins and reconciliation with God. Unless our sins are removed they will stand as an insurmountable barrier between us and God and block the way to heaven.

That we are all sinners is beyond question. Scripture confirms that there is not a righteous person on earth who does good and never sins. "All have sinned and fall short of the glory of God" (Romans 3:23). This is not a matter which we can ignore or treat lightly.

Nothing can be so disastrous as unforgiven sin because sin separates from God. Isaiah writes: "Your iniquities have separated you from your God; your sins have hidden his face from you, so that he will not hear" (59:2).

What a remarkably marvelous message of pardon is proclaimed in these words: "You have put all my sins behind your back." How cheering and comforting that God has forgiven the sins of his children so thoroughly as to remove them from his sight! The prophet Micah uses a similar symbolic expression to show how he removes them from his memory. "Who is a God like you, who pardons sin . . . ? You will tread our sins underfoot and hurl all our iniquities into the depths of the sea" (7:18,19). His forgiveness is full and complete. "For as high as the heavens are above the earth, so great is his love for those who fear him; as far as the east is from the west, so far has he removed our transgressions from us" (Psalm 103:11,12).

Note well that God's forgiveness is not limited or selective. He does not restrict his forgiveness to "little" sins. He casts ALL our sins behind his back. He casts ALL of them into the depth of the sea. He forgives ALL our iniquities. There is no sin so great that it cannot be forgiven. "Though your sins are like scarlet, they shall be as white as snow; though they are red as crimson, they shall be like wool" (Isaiah 1:18).

This does not mean that God winks at our sins or that he condones them. Rather, it means that his Son paid for them all with his own life. The forgiveness Jesus won for all and that God offers to all in the gospel is received only through faith. Those who are sorry for their sins and ask God for his pardon will most certainly receive it. The self-righteous, on the other hand, forfeit forgiveness because they will not acknowledge their need for it. "He who conceals his sins does not prosper, but whoever confesses and renounces them finds mercy" (Proverbs 28:13). Forgiveness is not license to continue in sin. It involves the responsibility to break loose from sin and avoid it. "Go now and leave your life of sin" (John 8:11) was Jesus' instruction to those whom he forgave.

The certainty of God's forgiveness is a priceless treasure which lifts the burden of guilt and punishment from us and assures us of peace with him now and hereafter.

> O faithful God, thanks be to Thee
> Who dost forgive iniquity.
> Thou grantest help in sin's distress,
> And soul and body dost Thou bless.
>
> O Lord, we bless Thy gracious heart,
> For Thou Thyself dost heal our smart
> Through Christ our Savior's precious blood,
> Which for the sake of sinners flowed.
>
> (TLH 321:1,3)

14.

A Conference with God

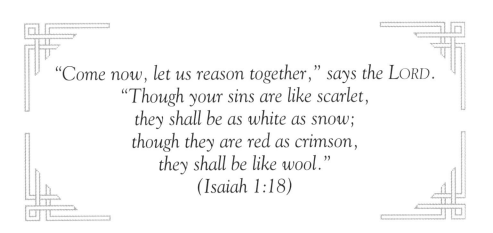

"Come now, let us reason together," says the LORD.
*"Though your sins are like scarlet,
they shall be as white as snow;
though they are red as crimson,
they shall be like wool."*
(Isaiah 1:18)

Conferences are the order of the day. Representatives of nations and political parties, business leaders, social leaders, management, and labor, all are taking part in an incessant round of conferences to iron out their problems and to enable people to live in peace and harmony.

It is indeed good that people should hold conferences with one another to relieve the tensions and to bring about greater harmony among themselves. But to achieve real and lasting success it is important that they recognize the underlying cause of all of mankind's troubled relations. People are at odds with people, and the world seems out of joint, because people are first of all at odds with their Maker.

That calls for a conference with God. And, indeed, the invitation for such a conference has been issued. God himself invites through the mouth of the prophet by saying, "Come now, let us reason together."

The principals of this conference are indeed very unequal. On the one side of the conference table we find the holy and righteous God, and on the other side his wayward and disobedient creature. On the one side, the almighty, omniscient, and eternal Ruler of the universe, and on the other side, the frail mortal, whose puny wisdom so often leads him into blind alleys, from which he can find no escape. But even though the conferees are far from being on a plane of equality, the invitation is not the rude summons of a stronger power to which the weaker must yield out of fear. Rather, it is a bona fide invitation to sit down and find a solution for the disrupted relationship between man and his Creator.

Except for God's gracious and reassuring words, "Come now," we might well approach such a conference with fear and trembling. But as dear children come with boldness and confidence to their dear father, so we may approach him, whom our Lord Jesus has taught us to address as "Our Father who art in heaven," with complete trust and confidence.

"Let us reason together" is his loving appeal. Our heart leaps in joyful realization. Our divine Creator reminds us of our crowning distinction which separates us from his other creatures. Man is the only creature with whom he can reason, the only one that has been created with the faculty to enter into a spiritual communion with him. And though this faculty has been corrupted by sin, God has not cast us aside; he continues to reason with us in order to salvage us and restore us to fellowship with him.

He plainly states the case: "Though your sins are like scarlet—though they are red as crimson." With guilt and shame we bow our heads and confess, "Yes, Lord, 'I know that nothing good lives in me, that is, in my sinful nature'" (Romans 7:18). We acknowledge that we have amply deserved God's wrath and displeasure, temporal death and eternal damnation.

But what a wonderful proposal it is that follows! Divine grace offers a way of deliverance, a cleansing from all unrighteousness. A change so marvelous and complete is offered that the soul dyed the deepest crimson shall become pure and white as the sparkling snow.

Obviously this change cannot result from God's ignoring sin and pretending not to see transgression. No crimson stain of sin is ever removed by ignoring it. No evil is ever made good by saying that it does not exist.

Can it be that God expects us to overcome sin and cleanse ourselves by our own power and works? If that were the case, the conference with God would have to break up in an atmosphere of hopelessness and despair, for we well know that complete and perfect purity could never result from our feeble efforts to fulfill the divine law. The spotted garment of our own righteousness can never be likened to the pure and sparkling snow.

How then shall that perfect righteousness be brought about? The answer is given by the prophet in the fifty-third chapter: "The Lord has laid on him the iniquity of us all" (verse 6). Jesus Christ, "the Lamb of God, who takes away the sin of the world" (John 1:29), has borne all of our sins and transgressions. By his perfect obedience and his suffering and death on Calvary's cross he made full atonement for all our sins and reconciled us to God the Father.

Forgiveness, perfect and complete, for the sake of Jesus, our Savior, is the proposal that is made to us in our conference with God. All sins are forgiven, great and small. No guilt is so crimson that it cannot be washed white in the blood of the Lamb.

Dare we spurn so gracious an offer? Can we leave the conference without gratefully receiving the blessing offered to us? Can we be satisfied to live in constant fear, in the cruel and heartless slavery of sin and Satan, when forgiveness and peace are so readily available to us?

The offer is without reservation. The benefit is without limit. But God does not force acceptance. Only free and willing compliance satisfies him. And that is what he asks.

> Oh, how blest it is to know:
> Were as scarlet my transgression,
> It shall be as white as snow
> By Thy blood and bitter passion;
> For these words I now believe:
> Jesus sinners doth receive.
>
> (TLH 324:6)

15.

God Hears Us

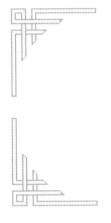

*This is the confidence we have
in approaching God:
that if we ask anything
according to his will,
he hears us.
(1 John 5:14)*

Prayer is one of the dominant features of religious service and is used by all who worship a deity. However, only proper prayer has any merit and must be directed to the one true God, the triune God, Father, Son, and Holy Spirit. To him alone such worship and honor is due, and he alone is able and willing to hear our prayers. Jesus answered the tempter: "It is written: 'Worship the Lord your God, and serve him only'" (Matthew 4:10).

In a world which is experiencing a critical energy crunch, prayer is the most neglected source of power. While it does not supply fuel to operate cars and run factories, it affords an abundant source of divine power for the asking. As Tennyson wrote: "More things are wrought by prayer than the world dreams of." As James puts it: "You do not have, because you do not ask God" (4:2). And he notes further that many who do ask do not fare any better because they ask with wrong motives (4:3).

This can happen in a number of ways. Often the necessary ingredient of faith is missing. "When he asks, he must believe and not doubt, because he who doubts is like a wave of the sea, blown and tossed by the wind. That man should not think he will receive anything from the Lord" (James 1:6,7).

Some prayers are offered in the spirit of dictating to God the time, place, and manner in which he should help. Prayer is not a blank check for the petitioner to fill out capriciously and then present it to God to be cashed. In that case man would rule the world and utter chaos would prevail.

Jesus warns that an unforgiving spirit kills prayer. "And when you stand praying, if you hold anything against anyone, forgive him, so that your Father in heaven may forgive you your sins" (Mark 11:25).

Many people *say* their prayers regularly and receive nothing. True prayer must come from the heart to be acceptable to God. Such a prayer is always answered. "This is the confidence we have in approaching God: that if we ask anything according to his will, he hears us."

What disturbs many sincere Christians is that their earnest prayers seem to go unanswered. They prayed fervently for this or that favor or blessing, and it did not happen as they requested, and they ask, "What was wrong?"

Let us rest assured that God does hear and answer every true prayer uttered in faith in the Savior's name, whether spoken with our lips or expressed by a sigh of the heart. But he answers in his own time, not always according to our wishes, but according to our needs. Some prayers are answered with a "yes" and quickly. Sometimes he answers with a "no" because he loves us too much to grant us our foolish or harmful requests. Sometimes he gives us bread when we ask for a stone. Often his answer is: "Wait a little while." He wants us to learn patience and trust. Sometimes he wants us to exercise our faith through trials and temptations and come out stronger through reliance on his power and wisdom instead of on our own strength and ingenuity.

When, in our distress, we plead with God to hear our prayers, it is necessary for us to "be still before the LORD and wait patiently for him" (Psalm 37:7). The answer is his, not ours, and it will always be right.

> Thine shall forever be
> Glory and power divine;
> The scepter, throne, and majesty
> of heaven and earth are Thine.
>
> (TLH 455:5)

Most often it is troubles and problems too difficult for us to handle that drive us to the throne of God in prayer, but our prayers ought never to be restricted to cries in distress. We enjoy countless reasons and times for expressing our deep gratitude to our Lord for priceless blessings of body and soul with songs of praise and prayers of thanksgiving. We need to heed the words of the psalmist: "Praise the LORD, O my soul, and forget not all his benefits" (103:2). It is our privilege and obligation to abound in prayers of praise and thanksgiving, knowing that they are in full harmony with his divine will.

> We'll crowd Thy gates with thankful songs,
> High as the heavens our voices raise;
> And earth, with her ten thousand tongues,
> Shall fill Thy courts with sounding praise.
>
> (TLH 13:4)

16.

O Lord! How Long?

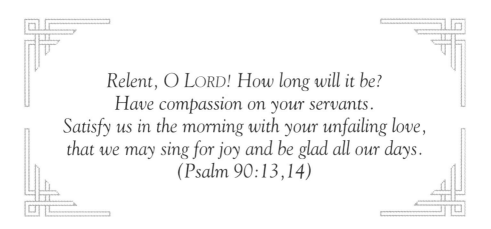

Relent, O LORD! How long will it be?
Have compassion on your servants.
Satisfy us in the morning with your unfailing love,
that we may sing for joy and be glad all our days.
(Psalm 90:13,14)

The Book of Psalms is often referred to as the prayer book of the Old Testament. The oldest in its collection of 150 psalms is Psalm 90, a psalm of Moses. It dates back to the time of the Exodus, when the Israelites were camping in the wilderness of Sinai. The closing verses constitute a prayer in behalf of the people participating in the Exodus.

While it was initially a prayer for a specific time and particular circumstances, its words have universal appeal and application and have found a place in the prayer life of the church. This is especially the case in lingering afflictions and prolonged problems and difficulties. When deliverance seems slow in coming, individuals as well as groups of God's people have often cried out in a mood of desperation: "O LORD! How long will it be? Have compassion on your servants."

The plea reflects a mixture of impatience and trust that God will respond favorably to his people because of his relationship with them. In spite of their weakness and failures and shortcomings, they still acknowledge his authority as their Lord, whom they want to serve. Because faithfulness belongs to his very nature, they are confident that the Lord will not spurn or reject them but will uphold his covenant with them. They cry out for an early solution to their adversity and appeal to his steadfast love to turn their laments into songs of joy and their distress into gladness.

There may be any number of things which may evoke such an outcry of misery, but there is no reason to abandon hope on that account. When we feel overwhelmed by the ordeal that has overtaken us and left us exhausted, it is the time to recall God's promise: "Those who hope in the LORD will renew their strength" (Isaiah 40:31). It may be a day of testing when our faith falters and our patience grows weak while we cry in anguish, "O LORD! How long will it be?" Then let us apply the words of the prophet Isaiah: "In that day they will say, 'Surely this is our God; we trusted in him, and he saved us. This is the Lord, we trusted in him; let us rejoice and be glad in his salvation'" (25:9).

The omnipotent Lord, who is the source of our strength, will supply all that we need and more if we will lean trustingly on him and bide his time to deliver us. With our strength replenished and our spirit refreshed, the future can be faced with renewed courage and confidence. Then we can rise above the difficulties that we encounter and can move forward with firm steps, a revived spirit, and joy in our hearts.

> Show us, Lord, the path of blessing;
> When we trespass on our way,
> Cast, O Lord, our sins behind Thee
> And be with us day by day.
> Should we stray, O Lord, recall;
> Work repentance when we fall.
>
> If our soul can find no comfort,
> If despondency grows strong,
> And the heart cries out in anguish:
> "O my God, how long, how long?"
> Comfort then our aching breast,
> Grant it courage, patience, rest.
>
> (TLH 226:3,6)

Acceptable Prayer

*May the words of my mouth
and the meditation of my heart
be pleasing in your sight, O LORD,
my Rock and my Redeemer.
(Psalm 19:14)*

Prayer is practiced all around the world by people of every class and nation. But to have value and meaning, it must be acceptable to God. It must come from the right source and have the right direction and goal.

The source of acceptable prayer must always be the heart of the petitioner. The mouth and the lips often participate in prayer but are not essential to it. Silent prayers are no less effective and acceptable than spoken prayers. But prayers that are only spoken with the mouth, often from habit, without coming from the heart, are not acceptable, no matter how beautiful they may sound. The Scripture says: "May the words of my mouth and the meditation of my heart be pleasing."

It is equally important for acceptable prayer that it have the right direction and destination. "May . . . [they] be pleasing in your sight, O LORD." Only the *Lord*, the one true God, Father, Son, and Holy Spirit, is able to hear prayers and respond to them. It is utterly futile to pray to idols, whether they be the work of men's hands, or even the work of God's creation, such as sun, moon, and stars, which some people blindly worship. No matter how sincere the idol worshiper may be in his invocations, their idols cannot respond. And it is just as futile to address prayers to saints by whatever name they may be called. They are not even aware of the prayers addressed to them. "But you are our Father, though Abraham does not know us or Israel acknowledge us; you, O LORD, are our Father, our Redeemer from of old is your name" (Isaiah 63:16).

Acceptable prayer will never make demands of God or prescribe to him how and when and where he must answer, but it conforms to "his good, pleasing and perfect will" (Romans 12:2). It follows the pattern of the Lord Jesus in the third petition of his masterpiece of prayer, The Lord's Prayer: "Your will be done on earth as it is in heaven" (Matthew 6:10).

The spirit of prayer is moved to action by various circumstances. At times it is gratitude for favors granted that evokes fervent prayers of thanksgiving. Perhaps an exuberant feeling of joy seeks expression in praise for the Lord of the universe. More often it is prompted by personal needs, such as the need for strength and redemption as expressed by the psalmist. Any or all of these can underlie acceptable prayer.

As long as we feel strong and self-sufficient, we can easily forget that our strength comes from the Lord and that we are dependent on him. As long as pride gives us the feeling that we deserve recognition for our noble intentions and good works, we will feel no need for a Redeemer, and our prayers will lack the essential quality that makes them acceptable to the Lord.

We do have personal needs and problems, and it is certainly acceptable to bring them before the throne of God in prayer. Indeed, "What a privilege to carry *everything* to God in prayer." But we should not become so absorbed in our personal concerns that we forget to include others. Paul writes: "I urge, then, first of all, that requests, prayers, intercession and thanksgiving be made for everyone—for kings and all those in authority, that we may live peaceful and quiet lives in all godliness and holiness. This is good, and pleases God our Savior" (1 Timothy 2:1-3). Jesus also taught us to pray with and for others in the OUR FATHER.

> You cannot pray the Lord's Prayer,
>   and even once say "I."
> You cannot pray the Lord's Prayer,
>   and even once say "My."
> Nor can you pray the Lord's Prayer,
>   and not pray for another.
> For when you pray for daily bread,
>   you must include your brother.
> For others are included
>   in each and every plea.

> From the beginning to the end of it
> it does not once say "Me."
>
> (source unknown)

Prayer is adaptable to time and situation. The mother in the kitchen, the father driving to work, or the child in the classroom, all can make their requests known to God by silent, heartfelt thoughts without interrupting what they are doing. At other times they may pause from their activity and offer a more formal prayer. They may accustom themselves to regular times for prayer as on rising in the morning or at bedtime. Before and after meals are excellent times to join with the family in prayer and thanksgiving. As members of the larger family of God, the Christian church, they will also feel the urge to say with David: "Glorify the Lord with me; let us exalt his name together" (Psalm 34:3).

Whether public or private, spoken or silent, acceptable prayer that comes from the heart and reaches out to our Father in heaven is a source of unlimited power and strength. It provides the assurance and comfort of divine help from a wise and loving Father to suit our best interests.

> Prayer is the soul's sincere desire,
> Unuttered or exprest,
> The motion of a hidden fire
> That trembles in the breast.
>
> Prayer is the burden of a sigh,
> The falling of a tear,
> The upward glancing of an eye,
> When none but God is near.

Prayer is the contrite sinner's voice
Returning from his ways,
While angels in their songs rejoice
And cry: "Behold, he prays!"

The saints in prayer appear as one
In word and deed and mind,
While with the Father and the Son
Sweet fellowship they find.

(TLH 454:1,2,4,6)

18.

Praise His Holy Name

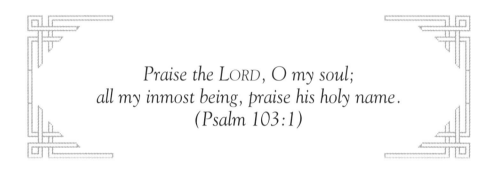

*Praise the LORD, O my soul;
all my inmost being, praise his holy name.
(Psalm 103:1)*

Unseal our lips to sing Thy praise,
Our souls to Thee in worship raise,
Make strong our faith, increase our light
That we my know Thy name aright.

(TLH 3:2)

A name is the distinctive medium by which we identify a person. The manner in which we use it reflects either favorably or unfavorably upon that person, because the person and name are inseparable. This is as true of the name of God as it is of our own names. Thus David, the sweet singer of Israel, gave glory to God himself when he sang: "O LORD, our Lord, how majestic is your name in all the earth!" (Psalm 8:1). Again, by calling upon us to praise the holy name of God, the psalmist is summoning us to praise and glorify God himself. The overwhelming awe and reverence we feel toward the holy and almighty God should manifest itself in the words addressed to him as well as in the language we use in speaking about him.

In yet another psalm David invites his fellow believers to join in his hymn of praise. "Glorify the LORD with me; let us exalt his name together" (Psalm 34:3). We too should joyfully participate in exuberant adoration of our majestic Lord God, for "holy and awesome is his name" (Psalm 111:9). He deserves such praise. When we look up to our exalted Lord with awe and wonder and give him praise with reverence and devotion, he graciously and generously bestows his divine favor upon us.

> From Him my life and all things came;
> Bless, O my soul, His holy name.
>
> (TLH 26:1)

To use this holy name carelessly or frivolously is not only disrespectful, but it is a shameful insult to the Giver of every good and perfect gift. How can we flagrantly misuse his holy name and expect him to smile upon us with his blessing?

The proper use of the name of God excludes spewing it out in anger when anything gets under our skin. It is likewise inexcusable to explode with the blessed name of Jesus when something goes wrong or surprises us. Whatever the excuse that is offered, thoughtless cursing and profanity are a sure sign that the person doing it has lost all reverence for God and does not understand or care about his wrath and judgment. It is not only disrespect, but contempt for the divine Lawgiver who says: "You shall not misuse the name of the Lord your God, for the Lord will not hold anyone guiltless who misuses his name" (Exodus 20:7).

When we use God's name with love and respect, we cannot use the holy name of God too often; but when we misuse it, once is too often.

> How sweet the name of Jesus sounds
> In a believer's ear!
> It soothes his sorrows, heals his wounds,
> And drives away his fear.
>
> It makes the wounded spirit whole
> And calms the troubled breast;
> 'Tis manna to the hungry soul
> And to the weary, rest.
>
> Jesus, my Shepherd, Guardian, Friend,
> My Prophet, Priest, and King,
> My Lord, my Life, my Way, my End,
> Accept the praise I bring.
>
> (TLH 364:1,2,5)

19.

Our Ministering Angels

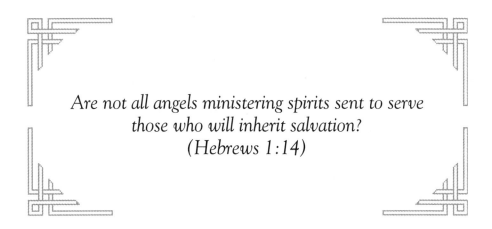

Are not all angels ministering spirits sent to serve those who will inherit salvation?
(Hebrews 1:14)

Our kind and loving Father in heaven bestows many precious blessings upon his children here on earth. Among the choicest of these is the presence of his holy angels to watch over them and to serve them.

Like God, the Creator, the angels are invisible, for they are spirits, and their activities cannot be observed by human eyes in our present state. Only very rarely did they become visible when they were given human form as they were sent out by God on special assignment. Thus on one occasion Abraham received angels as guests (Genesis 18).

Somewhat more frequently God caused his heavenly messengers to appear to his people with messages in visions. When Jacob was fleeing from his brother Esau and spent the night under the open sky with a stone for a pillow, he dreamed of a stairway reaching from earth to heaven with the angels of God going up and down, keeping constant contact with God. Thus Jacob was assured that wherever he might be, he would be as near to God as he had been in his father's house and that the angels would always be there to serve him (Genesis 28).

Being spirits, their movements are not restricted by time or space as ours are. Prison walls do not hinder their movements, and distance vanishes when God sends them on an errand.

Even though they lack a physical body, they are not weak. In fact, they are the "mighty ones who do his bidding" (Psalm 103:20). Neither Pharaoh of Egypt nor Sennacherib of Assyria were able to stand up to them. At God's command their great power may be used to carry out his judgments as well as bestow his favors and blessings.

The first line of duty of the holy angels is to serve their Lord and Maker by being his messengers and performing the duties he assigns to them. We behold an angel of the Lord announcing the birth of the forerunner of the Messiah to Zechariah (Luke 1:11-22) and the angel Gabriel announcing the birth of the Messiah to the Virgin Mary (Luke 1:26-38). And when the Christ was born, the angel of the Lord brought the glad tidings to the shepherds near Bethlehem and then joined the heavenly host to give glory to God in the highest for his wondrous gift (Luke 2:9-14). The sacred record gives many other instances where the angels served as God's messengers. They are also pictured as praising and glorifying their Lord around his throne.

Another major assignment given to the angels is to serve those who are to obtain salvation, that is, the family of God here on earth. God instructs them to keep watch over his children. "For he will command his angels concerning you to guard you in all your ways" (Psalm 91:11). What a vigilant and intelligent bodyguard these unseen companions become for them!

Jesus assures us that the angels share his special concern for the little ones in his kingdom. "See that you do not look down on one of these little ones. For I tell you that their angels in heaven always see the face of my Father in heaven" (Matthew 18:10).

Only those who "will inherit salvation" are included in these wonderful promises of God. All those who despise God and his holy Word place themselves outside of his family and the care and attention of his angelic servants.

Next to God, the holy angels are our very best friends, and we should be very careful not to grieve them and drive them away from us by godless behavior. They provide most commendable comfort and assistance when we are lonely or suffering or tempted. They are our helpers in trials and surround us in grief and discouragement.

Our gratitude for this marvelous gift of God can best be shown by striving, with power from on high, to do his will here on earth as it is done by the angels in heaven.

> We thank Thee that throughout the day
> Thine angels kept all harm away.
> Thy grace from care and vexing fear
> Hath led us on in safety here.
>
> Let angels guard our sleeping hours
> And drive away all evil pow'rs;
> Our soul and body, while we sleep,
> In safety, gracious Father, keep.
>
> (TLH 563:2,4)

20.

Die, Yet Live

*I am the resurrection and the life.
He who believes in me will live,
even though he dies.
(John 11:25)*

Death is a subject that few people care to talk about, and most like to change the subject when it does come up. Yet it is something that none can avoid or escape. In the midst of life we are in death. The indisputable statistic is that of all that are born, one in one will die, except for those living on Judgment Day.

> All men living are but mortal,
> Yea, all flesh must fade as grass;
> Only through death's gloomy portal
> To eternal life we pass.
> This frail body here must perish

Ere the heav'nly joys it cherish,
Ere it gain the free reward
For the ransomed of the Lord.

(TLH 601:1)

There are many things that keep reminding us that life is steadily moving on and that death is drawing ever closer. The setting of the sun and the changing of the seasons from spring and summer to fall and winter, the ripening of fruit and grain, the migration of birds, the departure of friends and relatives, even the constant ticking of a clock, all keep telling us that time is marching on and the grave is moving nearer.

But if that would be all that we had in prospect, that would be a gloomy outlook indeed. Then we could hardly fault the ungodly for saying, "Let us eat, drink, and be merry, for tomorrow we die."

Is death final? This is a question that has concerned mankind throughout recorded history. While some have concluded that death ends all, many others declare that it is impossible to know. However, the natural knowledge of God's law, written into the heart of man at his creation, bears forcible witness that the grave is not his final destiny. Abundant evidence of this is found in the manifold religions found upon earth; all teach some kind of future existence.

Some fifteen centuries before Christ was born Job pondered the question and asked, "If a man dies, will he live again?" (Job 14:14). In a firm and confident faith he answered: "I know that my Redeemer lives, and that in the end he will stand upon the earth. . . .

I myself will see him with my own eyes—I, and not another" (19:25,27).

The Redeemer came in the fullness of God's time in the person of Jesus Christ, the Son of God. It is he who makes the sublime claim and gives the glorious promise, "I am the resurrection and the life. He who believes in me will live, even though he dies." He has furnished indisputable proof of his claim by his triumphant resurrection from the dead on Easter morn, and he offers his victory as assurance of our ultimate victory. He has the power of life and death. He laid down his life as a ransom for our sins and took it again as infallible proof that he has conquered death. Because he died and rose again we can return to God and live forever.

Someone has said that death is not a period, but a comma. It is not the end—there is more to come. That which has lived and died can live again. Because Christ rose from the dead and became the first fruits of those who have fallen asleep (1 Corinthians 15:20), his resurrection will be followed by a bountiful harvest. All those who have died in faith shall be raised from the dead and be reunited with him in heaven forever.

> It is not death to die,
> To leave this weary road,
> And midst the brotherhood on high
> To be at home with God.
>
> It is not death to close
> The eye long dimmed by tears
> And wake in glorious repose
> To spend eternal years.

Jesus, Thou Prince of Life,
Thy chosen cannot die;
Like Thee, they conquer in the strife
To reign with Thee on high.

                (TLH 602:1,2,5)

Our Redemption

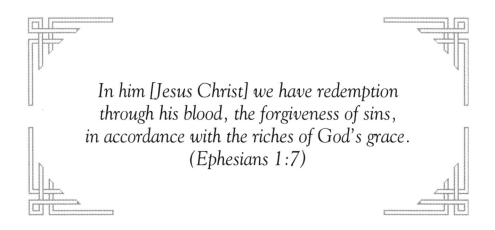

In him [Jesus Christ] we have redemption through his blood, the forgiveness of sins, in accordance with the riches of God's grace. (Ephesians 1:7)

> Redemption is purchased,
> Salvation is free.
>
> (TLH 278:1)

Thus Thomas Hastings in his popular hymn urges sinners to avail themselves of God's choicest gift to them.

Redemption of the sinner by the obedience and sacrifice of Christ is the central doctrine of the Christian religion. Christianity is the only religion that teaches salvation by the free grace of God rather than by human effort. All other religions have one idea in common—that man must contribute something toward his salvation and save himself by his own deeds, sacrifices, and prayers.

Redemption is the act of *buying back* some person or thing. The term is used by governing bodies and financial institutions for paying off bonds and securities, and by merchants for trading in coupons or making good on a special offer. It may also mean making payment to retrieve a pawned article, and even the paying of a ransom to free a captive. In the New Testament, redemption refers to our being rescued from sin and death by the obedience and sacrificial death of Jesus Christ, who for this reason is called the Redeemer.

Redemption always involves a price that must be paid. St. Paul reminds the Corinthian Christians that they were "bought at a price" (1 Corinthians 6:20). The more precious the object to be redeemed, the higher the price. Thus Scripture places a high estimate on our immortal soul when it declares, "The redemption of their soul is precious" (Psalm 49:8 KJV). Peter tells us how precious. "For you know that it was not with perishable things such as silver or gold that you were redeemed . . . but with the precious blood of Christ, a lamb without blemish or defect" (1 Peter 1:18,19).

Not only was it a great price that Christ paid, it was also a sufficient price for the whole human race. "For with the LORD is unfailing love and with him is full redemption" (Psalm 130:7). There is plenty for all, for the Lamb of God has taken away the sins of the whole world.

This great and perfect redemption was prefigured by the sacrificial offerings of the Israelites in the temple. These Old Testament sacrifices had to be repeated daily. Christ's redemptive sacrifice did not need to be repeated. "He entered the Most Holy Place once for all by his own blood, having obtained eternal redemption" (Hebrews 9:12).

The actual work of redemption was completed when Jesus cried out from the cross: "It is finished" (John 19:30). There is absolutely nothing that can be added or supplied. We have it. We own it. It is ours. The title is clear. It is an accomplished fact, yet at the same time it is also a coming event for us as we wait for the fulfillment of that redemption with Christ's second coming at the end of time.

Speaking of the last days, Jesus gave his disciples certain signs of the coming of the Son of Man and told them: "When these things begin to take place, stand up and lift up your heads, because your redemption is drawing near" (Luke 21:28). The complete enjoyment of that redemption is waiting for us as an inheritance reserved for us in heaven.

This great and precious gift, so dearly bought and so freely given, has come to us, not to hoard, but to share. The task is ours to pass it on. Our love for our Redeemer and for our fellow redeemed calls for a positive response. It compels us to be personally concerned that this redemption is freely proclaimed for the salvation of many others.

> Redeemer, come! I open wide
> My heart to Thee; here, Lord, abide!

Let me Thine inner presence feel,
Thy grace and love in me reveal;
Thy Holy Spirit guide us on
Until our glorious goal is won.
Eternal praise and fame
We offer to Thy name.

                ✳ ✳ ✳

Take my love, my Lord, I pour
At Thy feet its treasure store;
Take myself, and I will be
Ever, only, a11, for Thee.

                (TLH 73:5; 400:6)

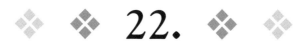

Salvation Is Free

*The gift of God is eternal life
in Christ Jesus our Lord.
(Romans 6:23)*

During the Spanish American War a number of Colonel Roosevelt's Rough Riders fell sick. When he heard that Clara Barton, the distinguished war nurse, had received a shipment of delicacies for the invalids under her care, Colonel Roosevelt asked her to sell some of them for the sick men of his regiment. His request was refused. Deeply concerned for his men, the Colonel asked: "How can I get these things? I must have proper food for my sick men." "Just ask for them, Colonel," was the reply. What could not be purchased could be had for the asking.

The mistake of Colonel Roosevelt, in attempting to purchase what was absolutely free, is one that is so often made in the matter of salvation. The great majority of people undoubtedly realize that the golden key of wealth, which will unlock virtually any door here on earth, is utterly useless to gain admittance into the mansions of heaven, and yet the notion prevails among many of them that they must offer something in return for eternal life. They will not hesitate to offer their own imperfect and inadequate righteousness to the holy and righteous God as a passport which should open the heavenly portals. It is imagined that the sincere effort to live according to the Golden Rule, the multitude of prayers offered, the good deeds done, or their pious conduct must somehow merit the favor of God.

Salvation is not a do-it-yourself project. Perfect obedience would indeed save a person, but nothing short of absolute perfection will satisfy the strict demands of the divine law. "For whoever keeps the whole law and yet stumbles at just one point is guilty of breaking all of it" (James 2:10). Since the fall of man into sin, no human except the God-man, Christ Jesus, has been able to render perfect obedience. St. John, the apostle, makes this very clear when he says, "If we claim to be without sin, we deceive ourselves and the truth is not in us" (1 John 1:8). And the psalmist testifies: "All have turned aside, they have together become corrupt; there is no one who does good, not even one" (Psalm 14:3).

It is futile to try to earn that which is beyond price, nor is it necessary, for Scripture tells us that eternal life is the gift of God. This priceless gift, procured by our Lord Jesus Christ, is freely offered to us in the precious gospel. However, it is not truly ours until it has been accepted by faith.

May the Lord preserve us from rejecting this gracious gift through pride and unbelief.

> Salvation free by faith in Thee,
> That is Thy Gospel's preaching,
> The heart and core of Bible lore
> In all its sacred teaching.
> In Christ we must
> Put all our trust,
> Not in our deeds or labor;
> With conscience pure
> And heart secure
> Love Thee, Lord, and our neighbor.
>
> Thou, Lord, alone this work hast done
> By Thy free grace and favor.
> All who believe will grace receive
> Through Jesus Christ, our Savior.
> And though the Foe
> Would overthrow
> Thy Word with grim endeavor,
> All he hath wrought
> Must come to naught,—
> Thy Word will stand forever.
>
> (TLH 266:2,3)

23.

The Open Heaven

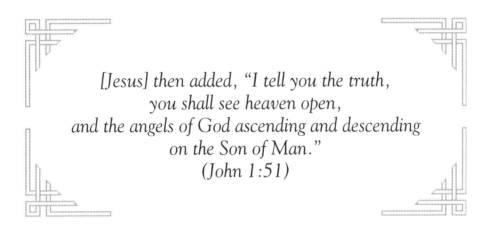

*[Jesus] then added, "I tell you the truth,
you shall see heaven open,
and the angels of God ascending and descending
on the Son of Man."
(John 1:51)*

These words of Jesus to Nathanael remind us of an ancestor of his according to the flesh, who, more than seventeen centuries before, had seen a vision of the open heaven. A lonely wanderer, who had left home because of an embittered brother, Jacob lay down to rest for the night under the starry canopy of heaven. He rested his head on a stone and so he fell asleep. Suddenly a glorious vision unfolded itself to him. From the very place where he was sleeping a ladder, or stairway, rose up, reaching into heaven, into the very presence of God himself. Ascending and descending upon this stairway to heaven was a host of angels, those heavenly messengers who serve both God and his children here on earth, keeping constant communication between God and his own people on earth. In the vision God himself promised Jacob his blessing.

When he arose in the morning, his loneliness and his fears had vanished. He now realized that no matter where he might go, he was as close to God and to heaven as he had been in his father's house.

This vision of Jacob, of heaven joined to earth by God, and of the portals of heaven standing open, has its ultimate counterpart in the promise of Jesus. While the saints of God in the Old Testament found heaven open to them because of their faith in the promised Messiah, it was the coming of Christ into the flesh which again opened heaven after man had willfully shut himself out of fellowship with God through sin.

The opening of heaven is an act of God. In the fullness of time he opened heaven wide and sent forth his only begotten Son down to us here on earth, to take upon himself our nature and to partake of our flesh and blood. Therefore we also like to sing at Christmas time:

> Praise God the Lord, ye sons of men,
> Before His highest throne;
> Today He opens heaven again
> And give us His own son.
>
> (TLH 105:1)

With a divine oath, "I tell you the truth," Jesus promised his disciples that they would see heaven open and the angels of God serving him who came down from heaven to bring salvation to the world. Thus the public ministry of Christ began with the promise of greater things to come, greater than the demonstration of his omniscience that they had just witnessed. Through him the enmity that existed between man and his Maker was to be abolished. The divine justice, which demanded perfect obedience to God's holy Law and satisfaction for evil done, should be fully satisfied. Forgiveness of sin and transgression should be procured, and heaven should be opened.

Jesus kept that promise. The mighty works that Christ performed—those countless miracles—gave convincing evidence of his direct contact with heaven. For the first time since the Fall the world saw a man, "the man Christ Jesus," who was able to keep all the exacting requirements of the law and to lead a life in this world of sin that was completely pure and holy, without any taint or blemish of sin. More than twelve legions of angels stood ready to obey his commands and to serve him.

Proof that his intense agony of body and soul, endured with patience and love for friend and foe, satisfied the demands of divine justice is found in his triumphant resurrection.

And since Christ did not suffer for his own transgression but was acting as our substitute, his victory has been proclaimed as our victory, and his merit has been credited to us as payment in full for our sins.

Through his blood shed on the cross he has reconciled all things to himself, and full forgiveness has been obtained for all and is given to all who accept it by faith.

Man's attempt to storm heaven by might and power will prove as futile as the ill-fated effort at Babel. His endeavors to *buy* his way in, either by wealth that he has acquired or by works of righteousness, will prove just as vain and useless. On the other hand, every humble and contrite sinner who in simple faith clings to the promises of Jesus will find the door of heaven opened wide to receive him or her, and see the arm of the heavenly Father outstretched in welcome to the mansions above.

> In heav'n above, in heav'n above,
> Where God, our Father, dwells,
> How boundless there the blessedness!
> No tongue its greatness tells;
> There face to face, and full and free,
> Forever, ever more we see
> Our God, the Lord of hosts!
>
> In heav'n above, in heav'n above,
> What glory deep and bright!
> The splendor of the noonday sun
> Grows pale before its light.
> The heav'nly light that ne'er goes down,
> Around whose radiance clouds ne'er frown,
> Is God, the Lord of hosts.
>
> In heav'n above, in heav'n above,
> God hath a joy prepared
> Which human ear had never heard
> Nor human vision shared,
> Which never entered human breast,
> By human lips was ne'er expressed,
> O God, the Lord of Hosts!
>
> (*The Children's Hymnal* 208:1,2,5)

24.

Headed for Glory

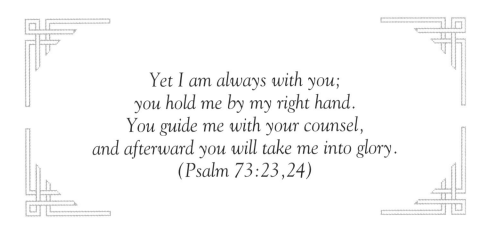

*Yet I am always with you;
you hold me by my right hand.
You guide me with your counsel,
and afterward you will take me into glory.*
(Psalm 73:23,24)

Where are you headed? What is the goal of your life? These are very personal and searching questions, and the answers reflect the priority of your values.

Many are propelled by a consuming inner drive for public acclaim. They strive to dominate some area of human accomplishment, endeavor, or pastime. They are determined to be acclaimed as NUMBER ONE in their specialty, whether that be on the playing field or in government, in business or in one of the arts. And if they can't be the greatest, they at least want to savor the honor of being in the top bracket.

Despite the great exertion in the heroic effort to achieve earthly fame and honor, they are won by only a few, and they are found to be so very fragile.

Others rate the accumulation of wealth and the prestige it produces as the measure of a successful life and the chief object to pursue. They may acquire it by tireless labor and special skills or by inheritance, and they often manage to keep and multiply it. But wealth is not without its problems and worries. There are the dangers of business losses and the peril of thieves and robbers. Besides this, the owners of great material treasure are also in jeopardy that their hearts might become too strongly attached to it, to their own great harm.

Still others are content to look for their fulfillment and happiness in a less competitive situation. They look for pleasant and peaceful surroundings without constant stress and strain. They are in harmony with Scripture, which states: "But godliness with contentment is great gain. For we brought nothing into the world, and we can take nothing out of it. But if we have food and clothing, we will be content with that. People who want to get rich fall into temptation and a trap and into many foolish and harmful desires that plunge men into ruin and destruction (1 Timothy 6:6-9).

But whatever the earthly circumstances or conditions of the Christian are: famous or forgotten, rich or poor, comfortable and satisfying or in trouble or distress, he is headed for glory that is infinitely better and more lasting than earth can ever offer. All who remain near the Lord and permit themselves to be guided by his counsel will be received into radiant glory by him to dwell with him in the Father's house. This is not a fleeting or fragile glory, for in his presence there is fullness of joy, with eternal pleasures at his right hand (cp. Psalm 16:11). Not only will their surroundings be unspeakably glorious, but the believers themselves will experience a great and wonderful change. Christ will transform their lowly bodies so that they will be like his glorious body (cp. Philippians 3:21). All the ills and woes of the body shall vanish. All the fears and frustrations of earthly life shall disappear. Heavenly peace and tranquillity will replace anxiety and unrest and tears.

Headed for eternal glory in heaven—what a blessed prospect! Cling to your Savior's hand to guide you safely there.

> I lay in fetters, groaning,
> Thou com'st to set me free;
> I stood, my shame bemoaning,
> Thou com'st to honor me;
> A glory Thou dost give me,
> A treasure safe on high,
> That will not fail or leave me
> As earthly riches fly.

* * *

> Guard, O God, our faith forever;
> Let not Satan, death, or shame
> Ever part us from our Savior;
> Lord our Refuge is Thy name,
> Though our flesh cry ever: Nay!
> Be Thy Word to us still Yea!

And when life's frail thread is breaking,
Then assure us more and more,
As the heirs of life unending,
Of the glory there in store,
Glory never yet expressed,
Glory of the saints at rest.

     (TLH 58:3; 226:8,9)

25.

Forgetting Can Be Good

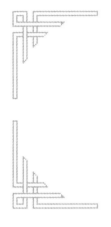

*But one thing I do:
Forgetting what is behind and
straining toward what is ahead,
I press on toward the goal.
(Philippians 3:13,14)*

How often we hear people lament and deplore their forgetfulness! They make it sound like a great catastrophe that they cannot remember certain things.

Most certainly the ability to remember is a precious gift of God that enriches our lives immeasurably. It enables us to store up our knowledge and experiences for future use and enjoyment. On the other hand, it is also essential to forget some things to be able to lead happy and productive lives. And we recognize it as a special blessing of God that we are able, at least in a measure, to forget the sorrows and troubles of the past. Time has a way of healing our hurts and bruises and diminishing our discomforts and disappointments.

People who cannot forget their griefs and grievances not only make themselves miserable and wretched, but they also pass their misery on to those around them and spoil their lives.

The apostle Paul had many bitter and painful experiences in the past as a missionary to the Gentiles. He also had haunting regrets for the harm he had done to the cause of Christ by persecuting his followers. But he did not permit the events of the past to depress his spirit or to hinder his activity. His letter to the Philippian Christians stated: "But one thing I do: Forgetting what is behind and straining toward what is ahead, I press on toward the goal."

He does not mean that the things which had occurred in the past, both good and bad, should or even could be completely erased from his memory. That would make it impossible for him to function effectively. Rather than reminding himself of these things constantly and being disturbed by them, he determined to put them aside so that he might give full attention to the things confronting him.

As in the case of the apostle Paul, there surely are things in our lives that we need to forget. Difficult and unpleasant circumstances happen in everyone's life. Jesus reminds us: "In this world you will have trouble" (John 16:33). We should not let them haunt us but forget them as much as possible.

It may be the evil deed that has been done to us or the spiteful word that has been spoken that we find so hard to forgive and forget. However, let us not lose sight of the fact that failure to forgive invites God's judgment upon ourselves, for "if you do not forgive men their sins, your Father will not forgive your sins" (Matthew 6:15). Perhaps we need to forget some mistakes and failures that we could have avoided, some indiscretions that we are ashamed of, or even a grievous sin that we deeply regret. Whether it is something that we have done or that we failed to do, it is not good to burden ourselves with accusing memories of past mistakes. If we humbly confess our sins, God will in love cast them behind his back to be forgotten (Isaiah 38:17).

Remembering and forgetting are abilities that God must provide. Unfortunately they are so frequently misused. We tend to remember what we ought to forget and forget what we ought to remember. In particular we so often forget the multitude of God's benefits and blessings, which he showers upon us so abundantly. Forgetting and remembering deserve our careful attention and correction wherever misuse is found.

> Lo, our sins on Thee we cast,
> Thee, our perfect Sacrifice,
> And, forgetting all the past,
> Press unto our glorious prize.
>
> (TLH 121:2)

26.

Profitable Affliction

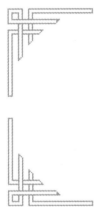
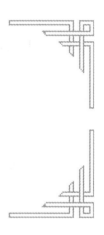

*It was good for me to be afflicted
so that I might learn your decrees.
(Psalm 119:71)*

Affliction is never pleasant or joyful, whether it be in the form of sickness, pain, or grief, or some other kind of sorrow or suffering. It troubles us, and we seek to avoid it whenever that is possible. But that does not preclude that it can be beneficial to us and therefore profitable. The psalmist says: "It was good for me to be afflicted." He confesses: "Before I was afflicted I went astray, but now I obey your word" (verse 67). Before he was afflicted he was inclined to depart from the Lord's ways and follow other ways. His troubles, whatever they were, taught him to pay closer attention to what God said in his Word and to be more faithful to the ways of the Lord. That was good and profitable for him.

He experienced what so many learn best in the time of trouble or need, that being down helps us to look up to the source of our strength and help.

The writer of the epistle to the Hebrews calls afflictions "the discipline of the Lord" and refers to them as the evidence of the Father's love for his children by correcting them. He compares this to the discipline of an earthly father by which he guides and trains his children so that they do not grow up as delinquents. Thus our heavenly Father's chastening is for our good, that we may share in his holiness (Hebrews 12:5,9,10).

Putting heartache and affliction into this perspective, we must recognize that they are not intended for our injury or harm, but for our ultimate good. They are a beneficial experience that the Lord lets us pass through for our spiritual growth. "Blessed is the man you discipline, O LORD, the man you teach from your law (Psalm 94:12). Solomon counsels wisely: "My son, do not despise the LORD's discipline and do not resent his rebuke, because the LORD disciplines those he loves, as a father the son he delights in" (Proverbs 3:11,12).

How often we fail to look upon divine discipline as a blessing! We do not like it. We feel that it hems us in and restricts our activities. It does not let us have our own way at all times. We are apt to become impatient and to complain and murmur. Sometimes we go so far as to resent it and to rebel against it. When this happens we lose sight of its purpose: to improve our conduct and behavior. "No discipline seems pleasant at the time, but painful. Later on, however, it produces a harvest of righteousness and peace for those who have been trained by it" (Hebrews 12:11).

Lives that are devoid of troubles and trials are usually dull and lack outstanding faith. Heroic faith is found where it has withstood the test of tribulation and drawn the afflicted child of God closer to the heavenly Father. Faith grows most luxuriantly where it has been watered by the tears of adversity. Such faith will bear abundantly the fruits of love and kindness, of patience and peace. In conjunction it will produce a deep inner satisfaction and joy.

> One there is for whom I'm living,
> Whom I love most tenderly;
> Unto Jesus I am giving
> What in love He gave to me.
> Jesus' blood hides all my guilt;
> Lord, oh, lead me as Thou wilt.
>
> What to me may seem a treasure
> But displeasing is to Thee,
> Oh, remove such harmful pleasure;
> Give instead what profits me.
> Let my heart by Thee be stilled;
> Make me Thine, Lord, as Thou wilt.
>
> (TLH 348:2,3)

27.

Beneficial Warning

*By them [the sacred Scriptures]
is your servant warned.
(Psalm 19:11)*

After praising God's Word for its matchless value and its many blessings, David, "the sweet singer of Israel," reminds us of another priceless benefit that it has for us. It also serves as a divine warning to keep us from evil ways and from the bitter consequences of sin and transgression.

When God delivered the Ten Commandments from the trembling, smoking Mt. Sinai, he called for honor and respect of his holy name, declaring: "You shall not misuse the name of the LORD your God." He added the warning, "For the LORD will not hold anyone guiltless who misuses his name" (Exodus 20:7).

At times the rebellious conduct of his people provoked the Lord to issue stern warnings. Their tendency to reject his authority and forsake him evoked the warning delivered through the prophet Azariah: "If you seek him, he will be found by you, but if you forsake him, he will forsake you" (2 Chronicles 15:2). Even stronger was the solemn warning delivered through the prophet Isaiah: "But rebels and sinners will both be broken, and those who forsake the LORD will perish" (1:28). Matching this is the Lord's warning through Ezekiel: "The soul who sins is the one who will die" (18:20).

Among the most repeated warnings in Scripture are those pertaining to the common human failure to remember and respond to the countless blessings that God bestows on us. Such is the message: "Praise the LORD, O my soul, and forget not all his benefits" (Psalm 103:2).

The danger of losing the proper perspective in values induced the apostle Paul to warn: "People who want to get rich fall into temptation and a trap and into many foolish and harmful desires that plunge men into ruin and destruction (1 Timothy 6:9). On the other hand, the apostle Peter warns us against letting down our guard against our archenemy when he writes: "Be self-controlled and alert. Your enemy the devil prowls around like a roaring lion looking for someone to devour. Resist him, standing firm in the faith" (1 Peter 5:8,9).

Many more warnings from the apostles and prophets of the Lord might be cited, but let us now listen to our Lord and Savior himself.

While Jesus was primarily concerned in revealing himself as the long-awaited Messiah, and teaching the way of salvation by precept and example, he did not neglect to warn his hearers about false teaching and sinful conduct. "Watch out," he told them, "for false prophets. They come to you in sheep's clothing, but inwardly they are ferocious wolves. By their fruit you will recognize them" (Matthew 7:15,16).

Lest people should become careless about remaining faithful to God and lose out because they are not ready to meet their Maker when he calls, Jesus warns: "Therefore keep watch, because you do not know on what day your Lord will come" (Matthew 24:42).

Mindful of the first and absolute need of the sinner, he also issues a very solemn warning against the all too common tendency, even among professing Christians, to be reluctant to forgive others or to carry grudges. "And when you stand praying, if you hold anything against anyone, forgive him, so that your Father in heaven may forgive you your sins" (Mark 11:25).

How grateful we should also be for this aspect of God's Word: its warnings! They, too, are evidence of the loving care and concern of our heavenly Father for his children, and they fulfill a very precious service for us.

> Rise, my soul, to watch and pray,
> From thy sleep awaken;
> Be not by the evil day
> Unawares o'ertaken.
> For the foe, well we know,
> Oft his harvest reapeth
> While the Christian sleepeth.

Watch against the devil's snares
Lest asleep he find thee;
For indeed no pains he spares
To deceive and blind thee.
Satan's prey oft are they
Who secure are sleeping
And no watch are keeping.

Therefore let us watch and pray,
Knowing He will hear us
As we see from day to day
Dangers ever near us,
And the end doth impend—
Our redemption neareth
When the Lord appeareth.

(TLH 446:1,2,6)

28.

Let Us Use Our Gifts

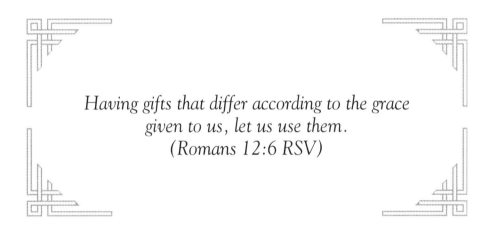

Having gifts that differ according to the grace given to us, let us use them.
(Romans 12:6 RSV)

Are we using the gifts that God has given us as faithfully as we should to serve and honor him? This is a question which has concerned Christians in every period of the history of the church. It was so in the apostolic age and still holds true today. In his letter to the Christians at Rome the Apostle Paul refers to that when he encourages them and us to make diligent and effective use of the Lord's gifts of divine grace.

To rouse the believers to greater activity and zeal in doing the Lord's will, the apostle shows them the possibilities available by listing twenty gifts and virtues with which the Lord has blessed his people. And while the gifts do differ in kind and in measure, each and every one of God's children possesses some of them.

Some have the gift of speaking God's Word while others can serve the church in various capacities. Some can teach while others have the ability to encourage. Some can share their earthly blessings with the needy, and others can give of their time and show kindness and perform acts of mercy. All can pray for others and show brotherly love as well as honor and respect. All can learn, with divine help, to be patient in trouble and rejoice in hope, to cling to that which is good and to hate evil.

A sincere and honest self examination may surprise us by revealing gifts of which we were not aware and refute some of the excuses that we are so quick to make. Too often we minimize our gifts and say, "I can't," when we haven't even tried. Too often we delegate the Lord's work rather than participate in it. We may envy the more gifted and declare that we are all thumbs and sincerely feel that is reason enough not to get involved and let our gifts go unused. Often the physically handicapped and disabled, the sick and bedridden, will put the strong and healthy to shame by their cheerful disposition and the rays of sunshine they cast on those with whom they come into contact. By the warmth of their smiles they convey peace and serenity to their surroundings. Their faith and trust in the love and mercy of God is reflected in the contented and joyous spirit they display. Who has not heard of physically blind people who have amazed those with perfect vision by their skill in using other talents? And invalids are not handicapped when it comes to prayer. Even the weakest are capable of sending silent prayers up to the throne of God, who assures us that he will hear them. Can we say, then, that we have no gifts or talents, or that they are too small to be of any value?

What a challenge the apostle here places before us to put our gifts and talents into the service of God! The motive should not be an attempt to obligate him to reward us for our effort, but our motive should be love and gratitude for the love and favor with which he has so richly blessed us.

The sincere desire to glorify our good and gracious Lord with our gifts and talents will also help to keep us from misusing them to glorify ourselves. Such an attitude interferes with their proper and God-pleasing use and is harmful to our soul.

When we feel overwhelmed by our own limitations, we should not forget the unlimited resources of divine help that are at our disposal for the asking in prayer.

> Let none hear you idly saying,
> "There is nothing I can do,"
> While the souls of men are dying
> And the Master calls for you.
> Take the task He gives you gladly,
> Let His work your pleasure be;
> Answer quickly when He calleth,
> "Here am I, send me, send me!
>
> (TLH 496:4)

29.

Serving with Gladness

*Worship the LORD with gladness;
come before him with joyful songs.
(Psalm 100:2)*

Serving God has numerous facets. For some it may be a career in answer to his call as he summoned the prophets and apostles to be his special spokesmen. Thus he still calls servants as full-time workers in the preaching and teaching ministries. However, these special servants of God are only leaders in the vast army of God's chosen people to help and guide them in serving their Lord and Maker. All of them, regardless of their calling or occupation, are duty bound to render service to him.

Our daily life offers a great variety of ways to serve God. This does not require special conditions or circumstances. We serve him when we are faithful in performing the duties of the calling into which we have been placed, whether in the church or in the world. This holds true when we occupy positions of authority and management or whether our status is that of followers or servants.

The apostle Paul instructed the Christians at Ephesus about this matter. To the servants he wrote: "Slaves, obey your earthly masters with respect and fear, and with sincerity of heart, just as you would obey Christ. Obey them not only to win their favor when their eye is on you, but like slaves of Christ, doing the will of God from your heart. Serve wholeheartedly, as if you were serving the Lord, not men, because you know that the Lord will reward everyone for whatever good he does, whether he is slave or free" (Ephesians 6:5-8).

Paul also had a word for the masters: "And masters, treat your slaves in the same way. Do not threaten them, since you know that he who is both their Master and yours is in heaven, and there is no favoritism with him" (Ephesians 6:9).

Opportunities to serve God abound all around us. Frequently they also occur apart from our regular occupation. Jesus suggests some of the ways we can do this when he speaks of the Final Judgment. Among the good deeds that he will acknowledge at that time are feeding the hungry, clothing the naked, visiting the sick, and giving shelter to strangers (Matthew 25:31ff.). Martha and Mary each served the Lord Jesus in her own way when Jesus was a guest at their home from time to time. Unexpected chances to serve God are also likely to present themselves to us.

Yet the most common and universally acknowledged form of serving God is through worship, both public and private. God expects such service and is pleased with it when it is gladly and sincerely given. To withhold worship in some form from him is to reject him as our Lord and God and is an affront to him. In our worship of the one true God we confess our dependence on him and pledge our allegiance to him. We praise him for the bountiful blessings that he has showered upon us and plead for his continued care and keeping.

To be truly God-pleasing, our service to the Lord, either through works or through worship, must be done with gladness. Where there is joy in serving, there is pleasure in being served. Deeds performed grudgingly are not blessed. Offerings brought with a feeling of compulsion are not received with divine favor. The motions of worship rendered with a sign of relief when they are over are not real worship at all.

God has given mankind a special gift to express gladness by singing, and we are exhorted to employ this gift in worshiping him. But even when the tongue lacks musical expression, or the situation is not favorable for an exuberant outburst of song, there can nevertheless be an exultation of God in the heart. He will understand it and be truly delighted with it.

> Ye lands, to the Lord make a jubilant noise;
> Glory be to God!
> Oh, serve Him with joy,
>   in His presence now rejoice;
> Sing praise unto God out of Zion!

Not we, but the Lord is our Maker, our God;
Glory be to God!
His people are we, and the sheep led by His rod;
Sing praise unto God out of Zion!

Oh, enter His gates with
    thanksgiving and praise;
Glory be to God!
To bless Him and thank Him
    our voices we will raise;
Sing praise unto God out of Zion!

(TLH 44:1-3)

30.

A More Convenient Season

> *[Felix] sent for Paul and listened to him as he spoke about faith in Christ Jesus. As Paul discoursed on righteousness, self-control and the judgment to come, Felix was afraid and said, "That's enough for now! You may leave. When I find it convenient, I will send for you."*
> (Acts 24:24,25)

Success or failure often depends on seizing the opportunity that comes along or letting it slip away by choosing not to grasp it. This not only holds true in the secular realm, but it applies to spiritual matters as well. The reason some people are lost is not because they never heard the saving gospel, but because they rejected its invitation and chose to go their own way. Such was the case of Felix and Drusilla.

Felix had been the Roman governor of Judea for seven years when he spoke the words mentioned above. His rule was marked by cruelty, greed, and corruption, and he was living in an adulterous marriage with a Jewish princess, Drusilla. Together they had heard much about the new believers in Christ, and their curiosity was aroused. The opportunity to satisfy their curiosity came when the chief captain in Jerusalem sent him a prisoner whom he had rescued from an enraged Jewish mob.

On his return to Jerusalem from his third missionary journey the Apostle Paul had been seized on the trumped-up charge of defiling the temple, and his enemies were determined to kill him for it. To protect him and give him a trial as a Roman citizen, Lysias delivered Paul to the governor at Caesarea. Although he was vindicated in a quick trial, because of some political maneuvering Paul was not released.

While he was in custody, Felix and Drusilla summoned Paul "and listened to him as he spoke about faith in Christ Jesus (Acts 24:24). When the apostle proclaimed the gospel in the context of the divine law and spoke of righteousness, self-control and judgment, Felix was troubled in conscience and shaken. He politely interrupted Paul and ended his exposition of the Christian faith. "That's enough for now! You may leave. When I find it convenient, I will send for you." The lesson was not too long, but too close and too hot for the governor.

What Felix really did by ending the lesson and excusing himself was to spurn God's hour of grace and to reject Christ as his Savior. There is no hint in Scripture or in history that the convenient season ever did come for Felix. Apparently he had no intention of giving Paul another opportunity to speak to his conscience in this manner.

Felix is long gone, yet he continues to speak to us that there is no more convenient season to give attention to the word of salvation than the present. The psalmist also says; "Today, if you hear his voice, do not harden your hearts" (Psalm 95:7,8). Elsewhere the apostle declares: "I tell you, now is the time of God's favor, now is the day of salvation" (2 Corinthians 6:2).

The same blessed gospel that brings life and salvation to those who open their hearts and accept it by faith can also be the source of death and damnation for those who do not want to believe, because they love sin and are not ready to break with it.

> Delay not, delay not, O sinner, draw near,
> The waters of life are now flowing for thee.
> No price is demanded; the Savior is here;
> Redemption is purchased, salvation is free.
>
> Delay not, delay not, O sinner, to come,
> For mercy still lingers and calls thee today.
> Her voice is not heard in the vale of the tomb;
> Her message, unheeded, will soon pass away.
>
> Delay not, delay not! Why longer abuse
> The love and compassion of Jesus, thy God?
> A fountain is opened; how canst thou refuse
> To wash and be cleansed in His pardoning blood?
>
> (TLH 278:1,2,5)

31.

The Truth

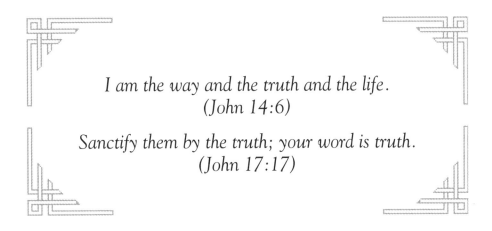

I am the way and the truth and the life.
(John 14:6)

Sanctify them by the truth; your word is truth.
(John 17:17)

In that crucial hour when Jesus Christ, the King of Kings and Lord of Lords, the only-begotten Son of God, stood on trial before Caesar's servant, the Roman governor Pontius Pilate, truth suddenly became the central issue. In defense of his unique kingship Jesus told Pilate, "For this reason I was born, and for this I came into the world, to testify to the truth." And then without any hesitation Jesus offered Caesar's servant citizenship in his kingdom without relinquishing his allegiance to his earthly sovereign. "Everyone on the side of truth listens to me" (John 18:37).

Scornfully Pilate brushed this gracious offer aside with the cynical reply: "What is truth?" (verse 38). He was a skeptic who dismissed the idea of absolute and unqualified truth as unrealistic. He abruptly closed the discussion and went out again.

Undoubtedly Pilate was aware that there were conflicting theories and philosophies on many subjects that were heralded as truth in his time. He concluded that it was impossible to determine which, if any of them, was correct. And then to have this rabbi, who was despised and rejected by his own people, tell him of the truth and challenge him with his proclamation of it was simply preposterous. He would have nothing to do with it.

This skepticism of Pilate regarding truth has been echoed and reechoed down through the centuries and is probably even more prevalent in our day. Many there are who insist that truth is relative, and question, if not scoff at, the claim of absolute truth. Philosophical speculation, often under the guise of science, claims special insight into truth, but the speculators cannot agree on the multitude of theories of where we come from, where we are going, the meaning of life and death, of heaven and hell, what God is like, and so on.

True science has opened many doors of knowledge to us, telling us how things work and why certain things happen. It has demonstrated how to split the atom and harness nuclear power. It has made great strides in medical research as well as in many other fields. But when it comes to spiritual things, it finds itself out of its element. There human wisdom and ingenuity must stop and let God open his Book and reveal his eternal truth to us. Jesus, the Teacher certified by heaven in the words: "This is my Son, whom I love; with him I am well pleased. Listen to him!" (Matthew 17:5), points to the truth in his high priestly prayer. He pleads with the heavenly Father in behalf of his disciples: "Sanctify them by the truth; your word is truth" (John 17:17). God's Word is truth absolute. It shows us the infinite wisdom and the loving heart of God.

This soul-liberating truth can be known. Jesus said to the Jews who had believed him, "If you hold to my teaching, you are really my disciples. Then you will know the truth, and the truth will set you free" (John 8:31,32). Jesus, the Word made flesh (cp. John 1:14), is identical with the truth. He is the truth personified. He declared, "I am the way and the truth and the life. No one comes to the Father except through me" John 14:6). He spoke the truth at all times, to friend and foe alike. To the unbelieving Jews he said, "If I am telling the truth, why don't you believe me? He who belongs to God hears what God says. The reason you do not hear is that you do not belong to God" (John 8:46,47). Those who believe and accept his truth will find rest and hope and eternal life with him.

> Thou art the Truth; Thy Word alone
> True wisdom can impart;
> Thou only canst inform the mind
> And purify the heart.
>
> Thou art the Way, the Truth, the Life;
> Grant us that Way to know,
> That Truth to keep, that Life to win,
> Whose joys eternal flow.
>
> (TLH 355:2,4)

Make the Devil Flee

Resist the devil, and he will flee from you.
(James 4:7)

When we mention the devil, we may very well find people who will regard us as being behind the times. To them the idea of a personal devil belongs to the Dark Ages and is outmoded for our own enlightened era.

But these people are themselves out of step with the ageless Word of God, which has a great deal to say about the devil in both the Old and the New Testaments. They likewise contradict our Lord Jesus Christ, who refers to the devil again and again. This is his description of the devil: "He was a murderer from the beginning, not holding to the truth, for there is no truth in him. When he lies he speaks his native language, for he is a liar and the father of lies" (John 8:44). In the Parable of the Sower Jesus alerts us to the devil's destructive activity: "Then the devil comes and takes away the word from their hearts, so that they may not believe and be saved" (Luke 8:12).

The devil, or Satan, as the leader of the evil angels who fell away from God is known, did not even shun to attack Jesus, the Son of God, at the beginning of his public ministry. Nor did his failure to ensnare Jesus deter him from advancing against his disciples. First, the devil had already prompted Judas Iscariot, son of Simon, to betray Jesus (John 13:2). Then he moved against Simon Peter, the boldest of the Twelve, to bring about his denial of the Master. Jesus warned, "Simon, Simon, Satan has asked to sift you as wheat" (Luke 22:31).

Wherever Jesus has followers they are in danger of the devil's assaults and must constantly be on guard. St. Paul warns the Ephesian Christians: "Do not give the devil a foothold" (4:27). Paul instructs them: "Put on the full armor of God so that you can take your stand against the devil's schemes. For our struggle is not against flesh and blood, but against the rulers, against the authorities, against the powers of this dark world and against the spiritual forces of evil in the heavenly realms" (Ephesians 6:11,12). The apostle Peter describes the devil as a roaring lion prowling around, looking for someone to devour (1 Peter 5:8).

Formidable as the devil is, there is no reason for us to throw up our hands in despair and surrender to him. He is by no means invincible. St. James assures us: "Resist the devil, and he will flee from you."

It is utterly futile to even imagine that this can be accomplished by either the drumbeats of masked devil chasers of primitive New Guinea tribes or by the charms and magic of a more cultured society. Neither can we rely on our own skill and strength as Peter sadly learned. We must use the means that God puts at our disposal. "Be strong in the Lord and in his mighty power" (Ephesians 6:10).

It is Jesus himself who gave us the finest example of combating the devil's temptations when he was attacked by the Evil One in the wilderness. He repulsed each attack with the Word of God. "It is written" (Matthew 4:1-11) was the key to his successful defense. God's Word is truth, and the devil, who operates by deception and falsehood, cannot stand up to it. With it we too can resist the devil and make him flee.

> Though devils all the world should fill,
> All eager to devour us,
> We tremble not, we fear no ill,
> They shall not overpow'r us.
> This world's prince may still
> Scowl fierce as he will,
> He can harm us none,
> He's judged; the deed is done;
> One little word can fell him.
>
> (TLH 262:3)

❖ ❖ 33. ❖ ❖

A Haunted House

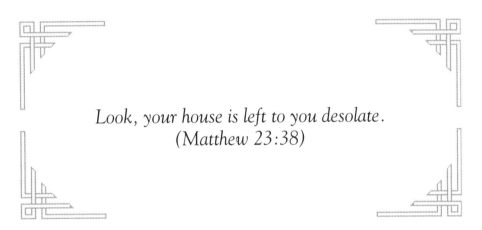

Look, your house is left to you desolate.
(Matthew 23:38)

How dreary and forlorn is a deserted, vacant house! The human occupants have left, and it stands empty and forsaken. The sounds and signs of habitation have given way to desolation. In place of voices, laughter, and weeping is the creaking of boards, the rattle of shutters, the flutter of bats, the scamper of prowling rodents, and the whistling wind.

What a startling and vivid picture for Jesus to employ in illustrating the withdrawal of God's presence and grace!

This remarkable statement applied first of all to Jerusalem, the center of Jewish life and worship. Jerusalem was a highly favored city in a favored land. King David made it a royal city, and from then on it had an illustrious history.

But better than its royal fame was Jerusalem's religious glory. Great prophets of Israel, including Isaiah and Jeremiah, taught in her. The temple, in which God's presence among his people was manifested in a very special way, stood there. Divine protection spared the city a number of times in extreme need and danger, and divine deliverance restored it after its destruction.

The greatest glory of all came to the "Holy City" when the Son of God made his appearance, teaching in the temple and market place and performing many mighty miracles. There he pleaded with the people to accept him, their long-promised Messiah, for their eternal salvation. But the Son of God fared no better than did God's prophets of old. He too was spurned and rejected by the very people he had come to help and to bless. With heartfelt sorrow Jesus, who but a few days before had shed bitter tears over the city, now laments: "O Jerusalem, Jerusalem, you who kill the prophets and stone those sent to you, how often I have longed to gather your children together, as a hen gathers her chicks under her wings, but you were not willing" (Matthew 23:37).

In these few words we find summed up all the long and tragic story of obstinacy of God's chosen people, of rebellion against their heavenly Father, of divine patience abused and divine love spurned. And now the measure of God's wrath was full, and his patience exhausted. Jesus foresaw that the crucifying of the Son of

God and defiantly calling his blood down upon themselves and their children would bring forth the fearful vengeance of God. Solemnly he exclaimed, "Look, your house is left to you desolate." With God, the rightful inhabitant, departed, the temple would no longer be God's house. The city would cease to be the "Holy City." When God would withdraw his grace, evil spirits would come into full possession. It would become a haunted house or, as Jesus calls it, a house forsaken and desolate.

Many of those living at that time were destined to see this dire prophecy of Jesus literally fulfilled by the destruction of the city by the Roman general Titus in A.D. 70.

The great tragedy of being left forsaken and desolate by God was not restricted to Jerusalem and the temple. Sadly, it applied also to many of the city's inhabitants. Instead of being the habitation of the holy God, they would become houses forsaken and desolate, haunted houses.

The same tragic circumstance confronts many people today. Obstinately rejecting Christ and spurning his compassionate love must lead to his withdrawal from their hearts. It inevitably results in emptiness, ruin, and perdition. When the Spirit of God withdraws from a person and another spirit enters in, then that person becomes a house left forsaken and desolate, a haunted house.

The solemn warning of Jesus was spoken in divine love, bidding all people to consider the dire consequences of forsaking their God and encouraging them to avoid the calamity of becoming a haunted house. The promise of God holds firm that none of them that take refuge in him shall be desolate.

> O God, forsake me not!
> Take not Thy Spirit from me
> And suffer not the might
> Of sin to overcome me.
> Increase my feeble faith,
> Which Thou Thyself hast wrought.
> Be Thou my Strength and Pow'r,—
> O God, forsake me not!
>
> O God, forsake me not!
> Lord, I am Thine forever.
> Grant me true faith in Thee;
> Grant that I leave Thee never.
> Grant me a blessed end
> When my good fight is fought;
> Help me in life and death—
> O God, forsake me not!
>
> (TLH 402:2,5)

34.

Hold Fast

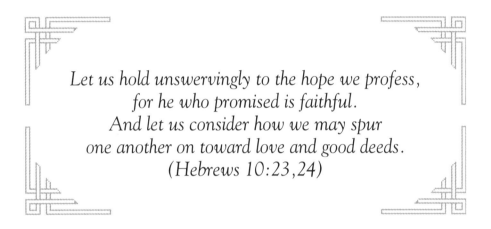

*Let us hold unswervingly to the hope we profess,
for he who promised is faithful.
And let us consider how we may spur
one another on toward love and good deeds.
(Hebrews 10:23,24)*

    The exhortation to hold fast or unswervingly implies possession of a worthy object to cling to and not give up. For the Hebrew Christians who are addressed here, that was the confession of their hope, which was solidly grounded on their Lord Jesus Christ and his divine Word. The charge was timely because they were exposed to many and strong temptations to surrender and abandon that hope. These included the clever assaults of Satan and the opposition of the world, which were at odds with God, as well as the inclination of their own hearts to be more concerned with what people thought than what God expected of them.

Time has not changed the need for such a mandate. It is as important for Christians today as it was in the first century of the New Testament era. We have the same basic problems. Temptations crop up on every hand. Satan is busy in many ways to divert us from our trust in and loyalty to our Lord and Savior. Satan endeavors to mislead us through a variety of false teachings and religious cults, and he appeals to our frustrations when we suffer from afflictions and calamities.

Satan has a willing and active accomplice in the ungodly world, which likes to heap scorn upon the Christians for their faith in Jesus. Furthermore, our own flesh and hearts tend to grow weary and are all too ready to give up. Rather than hold fast, we are inclined to throw up our hands in weakness and to surrender.

The importance of holding fast cannot be overemphasized. To become careless can result in giving up our hope for eternal life and surrendering to the powers of darkness. If we will only balance the blessings against the struggles and hardships that we are called to endure, it will prove the effort more than worth while. It will spur us on to cling to our Lord with all the power at our command. And when we begin to waver and to fear, we should remember that we are not alone in the conflict. God has promised: "So do not fear, for I am with you; do not be dismayed, for I am your God. I will strengthen you and help you; I will uphold you with my righteous right hand (Isaiah 41:10). And he who promised is faithful and will not abandon us in our need.

To hold fast is not a matter of choice. It is a God-given duty. It calls for steadfastness. It is not enough to confess the Lord for a time and then go our own way. It is a life-long commitment.

The members of the church at Smyrna in Asia Minor were given a command coupled with a promise by the living Lord. "Be faithful, even to the point of death, and I will give you the crown of life" (Revelation 2:10). Being attached to him for a while was not going to give them the crown of victory. It would not make them partakers of his glory. "But he who stands firm to the end will be saved" (Matthew 24:13).

Holding fast in the face of many temptations and difficulties is a test of our faith and love for Jesus. Relying on our own power we will not pass the test, but if we trust in God for strength we cannot fail.

> Let me be Thine forever,
> Thou faithful God and Lord;
> Let me forsake Thee never
> Nor wander from Thy Word.
> Lord, do not let me waver,
> But give me steadfastness,
> And for such grace forever
> Thy holy name I'll bless.
>
> Lord Jesus, my Salvation,
> My Light, my Life divine,
> My only Consolation,
> Oh, make me wholly Thine!
> For Thou hast dearly bought me
> With blood and bitter pain.
> Let me, since Thou hast sought me,
> Eternal life obtain.

And Thou, O Holy Spirit,
My Comforter and Guide,
Grant that in Jesus' merit
I always may confide,
Him to the end confessing
Whom I have known by faith.
Give me Thy constant blessing
And grant a Christian death.

                                    (TLH 334)

Personal Responsibility

The soul who sins is the one who will die. The son will not share the guilt of the father, nor will the father share the guilt of the son. The righteousness of the righteous man will be credited to him, and the wickedness of the wicked will be charged against him.
(Ezekiel 18:20)

Ever since Adam blamed Eve for his own sin, and she in turn tried to shift the blame, saying: "The serpent deceived me, and I ate" (Genesis 3:13), it has been the practice of fallen and sinful mankind to try to place the blame for their sin on someone or something else. All such efforts are utterly in vain, for the omniscient God holds all people personally responsible for their failures and transgressions.

The circumstances under which people live and the company they keep do indeed have a far-reaching influence for good or for evil upon them, but they do not excuse the breaking of God's law. He holds everyone personally responsible for his or her own conduct. His message is unmistakably clear and plain: "My son, if sinners entice you, do not give in to them" (Proverbs 1:10). "The soul who sins is the one who will die . . . the wickedness of the wicked will be charged against him."

Our relationship to God is always personal in every way. No one, except Christ, can take our place by assuming our obligations toward God or performing the duties for us which he places upon us. Neither bonds of friendship nor family ties will be of any avail when the time comes for us to stand in the judgment of God. No one can pull us past the eyes of the all-seeing God into the mansions prepared for his own. No one can substitute for us in the worship service. Clearly and distinctly God says: "Worship the Lord your God, and serve him only" (Matthew 4:10).

Our mother can render us many a service of love and devotion. She can nurse us in sickness and serve us in health. She can cheer us when depressed and pray for us in trouble or in need. But, with all her devotion and love, she cannot believe for us. She cannot accept the free grace of God in Christ Jesus in our behalf, for "the righteous will live by *his* faith" (Habakkuk 2:4). The "faith of our fathers" was their hope and salvation, but will benefit us only if we follow in their footsteps on the heaven-bound way.

"So then, each of us will give an account of himself to God" (Romans 14:12). That means that we will have to answer to God for our conduct as well as the use we have made of our time, talents, and all the other things that he has put into our care, whether they be few or many. How we use them to his glory and the welfare of others as well as ourselves is of concern to him. He holds us responsible for them and requires us to give an account to him of how we use them.

It will not work to try to excuse our neglect of responsibility by referring to the example of our neighbor. When Jesus had restored Peter to his apostleship after he had denied his Lord (John 21:15ff.), Peter saw the disciple John nearby and asked: "Lord, what about him?" (verse 21) Gently, but firmly, Jesus explained that the faithfulness or failure of another could not alter his responsibility. "If I want him to remain alive until I return, what is that to you? You must follow me" (verse 22).

As we reflect on our failures and transgressions of the past in the light of our responsibilities, we can only cast ourselves upon the boundless mercy and love of God and plead that he forgive us through the blood of Christ, which cleanses us from all sin.

Aware of our weakness, we recall the gracious promise of God: "My power is made perfect in weakness" (2 Corinthians 12:9). Embracing this promise, we can go forward with confidence to assume our responsibilities with his help.

> Sing, pray, and keep His ways unswerving,
> Perform thy duties faithfully,
> And trust His Word; though undeserving,
> Thou yet shalt find it true for thee.
> God never yet forsook in need
> The soul that trusted Him indeed.

(TLH 518:7)

As Long as It Is Day

> *As long as it is day, we must do the work of him who sent me. Night is coming, when no one can work.*
> *(John 9:4)*

With one master stroke Jesus explains the need for himself and his followers to be about the heavenly Father's business. Referring to one of the most common and familiar occurrences in nature—the coming of the night—Jesus compares it to a solemn and obvious experience that everyone must face sooner or later, that the time to work has expired. That is a plain and simple fact which no one can deny. There is no question that it is coming. As surely as the rising sun is followed by its setting again in the evening, just so certainly will our earthly life draw to a close and its activity come to an end.

Time marches on. It is folly for us to ignore this truth or even to deny it. Rather, we ought to give it most careful consideration in our daily planning.

"As long as it is day," Jesus says. We catch a note of urgency in the message. The time is limited and brief. There is none to be wasted. When Jesus spoke these words he had less than six months left in which to work before he sacrificed himself on Calvary's cross for us. We cannot know how long before we will be asked to lay down our working instruments and be summoned out of this life. In poetic language the psalmist likens the length of our days to grass and the flowers of the field when that is compared with the eternal existence of God (Psalm 103:14-17).

The night is coming. It is not here yet. It is still day to use and enjoy. The opportunity to work and to serve our Lord and Master is still here. Just keeping active and going through a lot of motion is not enough. Our activity should have the higher purpose of being "God's fellow workers" (1 Corinthians 3:9) in the building of his kingdom. Other things that we do may well have value for a time, but what is done for the Lord's kingdom has truly lasting worth. It may not win the applause of men, but it will bring a much higher reward, the "well done" of our Lord, and will bear fruit for eternity.

The night is coming. We cannot hinder or delay its appearance or stall for time. It will not wait for our convenience. It behooves us to work as long as it is day. "I tell you, now is the time of God's favor, now is the day of salvation" (2 Corinthians 6:2).

The child of God can face the night of death with trust and confidence because Christ has conquered death by his death and resurrection. Now death is only a shadow of its former self. With David we can joyfully sing: "Even though I walk through the valley of the shadow of death, I will fear no evil, for you are with me; your rod and your staff, they comfort me" (Psalm 23:4). With Simeon of old the believers can depart in peace in the knowledge that the Savior of the world has come and brought salvation for all people.

For those who have fellowship with Christ, a new morning will dawn in the mansions of the Father's house, where the ascended Christ has gone to prepare a place for them. There they will rest from their labors and dwell with saints and angels in everlasting blessedness.

> Hark! the voice of Jesus crying,
> "Who will go and work today?
> Fields are white and harvests waiting,
> Who will bear the sheaves away?"
> Loud and long the Master calleth,
> Rich reward He offers thee;
> Who will answer, gladly saying,
> "Here am I, send me, send me"?
>
> Let none hear you idly saying,
> "There is nothing I can do,"
> While the souls of men are dying
> And the Master calls for you.
> Take the task He gives you gladly,
> Let His work your pleasure be;
> Answer quickly when He calleth,
> "Here am I, send me, send me!"
>
> (TLH 496:1,4)

37.

The Final Victory

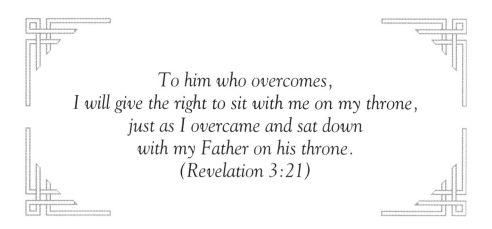

*To him who overcomes,
I will give the right to sit with me on my throne,
just as I overcame and sat down
with my Father on his throne.
(Revelation 3:21)*

The ecstasy of victory is among the most thrilling emotions that we can have. It is the enjoyment of winning the prize in an all-out effort of a hard-fought contest. Without confrontation there can be no victory, and the more strenuous the conflict, the sweeter and more satisfying the victory.

Life presents us with many situations or opportunities which test our skill and our will as well as our endurance, which determine whether we become winners or losers. Some situations are thrust upon us, while others are of our own choice. Among the latter are the variety of athletic contests that are so popular among us. The greater the rivalry and the stronger the competition, the more glorious and exhilarating the victory.

On the other hand, most people are confronted with struggles and contests that are not fought on the playing field in front of cheering crowds. These struggles are much less visible and usually go unnoticed. For this reason they require as much or more courage and endurance to attain the victory. Such may be the ongoing battle with temptations to evil that come from within and from without. It may be the struggle to make a good and honest living for oneself and loved ones amid misfortunes and adversities. In any case, the victory, whether noticed or not, can be very satisfying.

The victories that beckon are as varied as the times and circumstances. They may be no more important than winning a friendly game, or they may leave their mark on the course of history.

There is, however, one victory that is of supreme importance for everyone of us, and that is the final victory over sin, death, and the powers of darkness. This is the victory which God promises to all who remain faithful to the end. "Be faithful, even to the point of death, and I will give you the crown of life" (Revelation 2:10). It is the victory over the last enemy, death itself. "He will swallow up death forever. The Sovereign LORD will wipe away the tears from all faces" (Isaiah 25:8).

The rapture and joy of this victory far surpasses our ability to fully comprehend and describe it. We let our Lord Jesus assist us through his words: "To him who overcomes, I will give the right to sit with me on my throne, just as I overcame and sat down with my Father on his throne."

Because our Lord and Savior triumphantly overcame the last foe on Calvary, we too can now overcome and obtain the final glorious victory. With the apostle Paul we can say: "But thanks be to God! He gives us the victory through our Lord Jesus Christ" (1 Corinthians 15:57).

> Rise, ye children of salvation,
> All who cleave to Christ, the Head.
> Wake, arise, O mighty nation,
> Ere the foe on Zion tread.
> He draws nigh and would defy
> All the hosts of God Most High.
>
> Saints and heroes long before us
> Firmly on this ground have stood;
> See their banner waving o'er us,
> Conqu'rors through the Savior's blood.
> Ground we hold whereon of old
> Fought the faithful and the bold.
>
> Fighting, we shall be victorious
> By the blood of Christ, our Lord;
> On our foreheads, bright and glorious,
> Shines the witness of His Word;
> Spear and shield on battlefield,
> His great name we cannot yield.
>
> When His servants stand before Him,
> Each receiving his reward;
> When His saints in light adore Him,
> Giving glory to the Lord,
> "Victory!" our song shall be
> Like the thunder of the sea.
>
> (TLH 472)